THE MODERN FASCIST HANDBOOK

THE MODERN FASCIST HANDBOOK

a primer on the will to power

FRED B. DAVIS

Erudite First Editions

COPYRIGHT

The Modern Fascist Handbook

Copyright 2023 Fred B Davis

All Rights Reserved. No part of this book may be reproduced or used in any manner without the permission of the copyright owner except for brief quotations in a book review.

Paperback ISBN: 978-1-0881-8786-9
E-book ISBN: 978-1-0881-8793-7

first edition 2023
10 9 8 7 6 5 4 3 2 1
manuscript in Times New Roman 12pt

Fred B Davis
Non-Fiction   Erudite First Editions

Contents

COPYRIGHT v

1	INTRODUCTION	1
2	RECENT HISTORY OF FASCISM	12
3	PRINCIPLES OF FASCISM	33
4	EVENTS A FASCIST LEADER WILL ENCOUNTER	48
5	THE PERSONAL TOUCH	74
6	SELECT QUOTATIONS FROM 2022	92
7	CONCLUSIONS & EXECUTIVE SUMMARY	108
8	SIXTEEN AMERICAN ILLUSIONS	114
9	POSTSCRIPT: TALKING POINTS	124

Chapter 1

INTRODUCTION

For the past 75 years, fascism has been out of favor in America. We attacked fascism in all its forms, from the overt Nazi party in WWII to the Klu Klux Clan and McCarthy Communist witch hunts in the 1950s. Not all of us. And not every time.

For the balance of recorded history, in nations outside America, fascism has been the norm. The strong lead the weak and take the lion's share of the rewards. Dictatorships, Monarchy, Aristocracy, etc. These are the norms of human societies.

The simple reason is fascism works.

Most politicians who seek power are given Machiavelli as required reading. Yet much like Shakespeare, he was a man of his century. Much is lost in translation. Instead of half-comedic farce and veiled weak metaphors seen from today, Machiavelli was a very direct and very valuable guide when read by the men of his time. Those lessons still work.

The American Founders warned about this moment in American history. Students of history themselves, they knew the inherent weakness of a republic masquerading as a democracy. In Federalist Papers No. 10, James Madison wrote of the threat of "faction," which he defines as "a number of citizens, whether amounting to a majority or a minority of the whole, who are united and actuated by some common impulse of passion, or of interest, *adverse to the rights of other citizens*, or the permanent and aggregate *interests of the community*."

Madison believed that a *constitutional republic* would serve as a bulwark against faction: "The influence of factious leaders may kindle a flame within their particular States, but will be unable to spread a general conflagration through the other States." He was proven wrong when the Confederate states created a separate nation. Yet that was far before modern methods of influence, psychology, and mass media. Many nations have attempted variations on implementing Madison's viewpoint to protect the rights of their citizens and the interest of their communities. It has been to this day the greatest political contribution by America to the cause of freedom of worship & opinion worldwide.

In America today, it is this system that you must overcome to take power. True power. There are flaws and openings in the freedoms offered within such a system that can be exploited. In the 2022 midterm congressional and governor elections, fascists advanced but failed to generate a 'red wave' of victory by pulling back on the principles detailed in this volume. Take note of their half-measures or be cast aside.

In the 21st century, new political figures have the advantage of written recorded history, in some detail, of several centuries of political movements and philosophies, not to mention ancient Greek and Roman models. Identification of a philosophy that you can wholeheartedly embrace is critical to the successful political figure, for in this manner, the required *consistency* is achieved. Without consistency, those who are natural followers will not trust that you are just telling them what they wish to hear (like regular politicians of every party in every country). It is *consistency & passion* which persuade, not ethics or morals. Some will follow your principles, and others will never do so. The trick is to have your base of supporters *rabidly* embrace you as the embodiment of whatever political movement or philosophy you espouse. Especially fascism, which ironically limits their own freedoms.

This is the core reason democracy always fails. Liberal do-gooders are universally despised as weak, even by those they attempt to serve. Empires and regime change are built on authoritarianism.

Carl Sagan wrote prophetically in 1997, "I have a foreboding of an America in my children's or grandchildren's time - when the United States is a service and information economy; when nearly all the manufacturing industries have slipped away to other countries; when awesome technological powers are in the hands of a very few, and no one representing the public interest can even grasp the issues; when the people have lost the ability to set their agendas or knowledgeably question those in authority; when clutching our crystals and nervously consulting our horoscopes, our critical faculties in decline, unable to distinguish between what feels good and what's true, we slide, almost without noticing, back into superstition and darkness..." What an intelligent and perceptive man. Too soft-hearted to become a political leader, he was and is respected for his applied intellect.

He described the dumbing down of Americans as most evident in the slow decay of substantive content in enormously influential media, the 30-second sound bites (now down to 10 seconds or less, and done by amateurs), lowest common denominator programming, credulous presentations on pseudo-science and superstition, but especially a kind of *celebration of ignorance*. Fertile ground in which fascism of all forms may flourish.

This is the first lesson for the modern fascist. You do not actually have to be a believer yourself, but much like priests and other religious shamans, it is essential you *appear* to be. In fact, the parallels between assembling a cult and a political movement are significant. Cults are often dismissed by established religions or political parties, yet *they each started* that way. It is only by surviving the founder that a cult gains the status of a 'true' religion or political party. Be remembered.

Nevertheless, sets of principles are critical. Again, you will not 'convert' or 'subvert' everyone into being a follower, so *do not try*. Those who want to follow must be given a consistent doctrine to embrace. Herein, we organize this handbook based on outlining a variety of solid fascist principles, not abstract dogma. Not weak words of universal brotherhood and welfare. These principles are then expanded by applying them to a variety of political events which you shall face. Lastly, specific examples of recent effective leaders are presented to clarify how to make any event work for you and frustrate an amazed opposition. Democrats are tailor-made for this role. You do not always have to win - just sow enough doubt in the minds of followers, and they will continue to support you enough to fight another day.

Historically, the term fascist or fascism refers to an authoritarian and nationalistic 'right-wing' system of government and social organization. These are characterized by dictatorial power, forcible suppression of opposition, and strong regimentation of society and the economy in a manner that came to prominence in early 20th-century Europe. It was found that even among people with no prior exposure to fascism, a significant percentage of the general public *will always agree* with many, if not all, of its principles.

After all, does society everywhere not have rules

enforced by an authority? Are not the peoples of the world organized into nations whose citizens take *rightful pride* in their nation? Do not all living creatures and nations actively oppose any who will undermine *them*, *their* nation, or *their* authority? And who would disagree with a leader who opposes chaos in favor of rules of behavior, *law, and order*, both private and economical, to maintain order and security? To promote the national welfare and *show favoritism to our own people* over people in other nations?

For those who may think this tome is designed for the few of privilege, the rich spoiled son of Fred Trump, or the inherited power base of the Castros or the KGB's Putin, allow me to dissuade you of that notion. The lessons imparted herein can and should be applied by supporters right down the line to the frontline workers in, say, a deep blue state where he or she has little open power. They do have power: the ability to throw sand in the opposition's machinery. To delay, evade, and criticize their every move. To point out their every actual mistake, not just your negative spin on decent or logical programs or actions.

Yes, many are those who will agree with these fascist stances. The true fascist leader will not be distracted by the welfare of his own people as the primary goal but will take these logical platforms and extend them to ensure continuation of his own power, which is the only meaningful goal for such a leader. Do you have that strength? As a winner, can you swim against the media tide until history breaks for a moment in your favor? A moment will be all it takes as your opposition continues to murmur, "It cannot happen here," while they are swept away.

The lessons of history, especially recent history, are the source material for this manual which will train and guide the next gladiators in their quest for power. Understand that if you fail, you will be vilified and remembered by history as a criminal, so do not hold back on any effort to gain or retain power.

There is no return from this path.

Observe the turn from 2 parties with differing principles to America after 2012. CNN host John King asked candidate Newt Gingrich about claims by one of his ex-wives (Gingrich has been married three times) that he pressed her in 1999 to have an open marriage. Not answering, Gingrich responded by condemning the "destructive, vicious, negative nature of much of the news media," declared that he was "appalled" that King would begin a presidential debate on the topic, and said that it was "despicable" for King to make Gingrich's ex-wife's claim an issue two days before a Republican primary.

The crowd interrupted Gingrich with cheers and hoots of approval. But why? Wasn't King's underlying question fair? After all, Gingrich had admitted to cheating on his first and second wives, and he admitted to cheating on his second wife at the same time that he was speaker of the House and leading impeachment proceedings against President Bill

Clinton for lying under oath about his own extramarital affairs.

Moreover, Gingrich was having his affair after the Southern Baptist Convention, the largest Protestant denomination in America and a key Republican constituency, had passed a Resolution on the Moral Character of Public Officials that contained the following statement: "Tolerance of serious wrong by leaders sears the conscience of the culture, spawns unrestrained immorality and lawlessness in the society, and surely results in God's judgment."

Surely, heavily evangelical voters in a key Republican stronghold would be concerned about Gingrich's scandals? A man who cheats on marriage vows to God will surely cheat us. No, they were far angrier at media outlets than they were at any Republican hypocrisy.

Gingrich went on to win the South Carolina primary in a "landslide" powered by evangelicals. It was the only time in primary history that South Carolina voters failed to vote for the eventual GOP nominee. But South Carolina voters weren't out of step; rather, they were ahead of their time. They forecast the Republican *break with character* in favor of a man who would "fight."

To understand the emotional and psychological aftermath of Senator Mitt Romney's irrelevance, one has to look at the cultural break between the GOP establishment—which commissioned an "autopsy" of the party in 2012 that called for greater efforts at inclusion—and a grassroots base that was convinced that it had been hoodwinked by party leaders into supporting the "safe" candidate.

They wanted a street brawler, and when (they believed) Romney campaigned with one hand tied behind his back, they were angry. Yes, there was anger at Democrats and reporters for their treatment of Romney, but the raw anger that really mattered was their anger at Romney for the way he treated Obama and the press. They were furious that he didn't angrily confront Candy Crowley when she famously fact-checked him in the midst of the third and final presidential debate of 2012.

And so the Republican establishment and the Republican base moved apart, with one side – professionals - completely convinced that Romney lost because he was perhaps, if anything, too harsh (especially when it came to immigration) and the other – the base - convinced that he lost because he was too soft.

Trump's nomination was a triumph of that base. Well before Romney came out against Trump in the primary and well before Romney's first impeachment vote, Trump supporters scorned him. They despised his alleged weakness.

When Trump won, the base had its proof of concept. Fighting worked, and not even Trump's loss—along with the loss of the House and the Senate in four short years—has truly disrupted that conclusion. And why would it? Many millions still don't believe he lost.

The Mitt Romney martyr theory thus suffers from a fatal defect. It presumes that large numbers of Republicans weren't radicalized before Romney's rough treatment. In truth, they already hated Democrats and the media, and when Romney lost, their message to the Republican establishment in 2016 was just as clear as it was in South Carolina in 2012. No more nice guys. The "character" that mattered was a commitment to punching the left directly in the mouth.

Expanding on that anti-democratic theme, attacking 1 man 1 vote, is Pastor Shane Vaughn. In five out of the past 58 U.S. presidential elections, the winner did not win the popular vote – that includes the past two Republican presidents, but won because of the Constitution's Electoral College. Pastor Vaughn says he has had "a stroke of genius" and wants the election of U.S. Senators to bypass U.S. citizens and be decided by an "Electoral College" in each state.

Far-right Rep. Marjorie Taylor Greene (R-Ga.) referred to the various GOP factions that are meeting weekly to discuss strategy for when Republicans take control of the House of Representatives as the mafia in its heyday. "The five families, you know the reference, the five families are parts of our conference, all the different parts," the extremist congresswoman told former Trump White House chief strategist Steve Bannon on his "War Room" show. For those of you who doubt this handbook, think back on the handful of families which founded the Roman empire in just this manner. Who founded America itself. Remember.

It doesn't take many if they have a clear vision and are ruthless.

"We are coming together and having discussions on how we are going to govern," said Greene.

Chapter 2

RECENT HISTORY OF FASCISM

<u>1776 Project</u>

A report issued by President Trump in 2020 details his interpretation of the philosophy which was in place at the founding of America: racism & fascism. The founders of America who broke off in a civil war with Great Britain were all aristocrats, many wealthy, somewhat educated, but all accomplished men of the colonies. It is the slaughter of the natives and black slavery very upon which America was founded, with the rich getting richer and the poor (even those not technically slaves) remaining serfs. The founders believed in the elite telling the masses what to think and how to live.

The masses themselves have always believed this and cling to strong leaders.

President Trump formed the commission saying that American heritage was under assault by revolutionary fanatics and that the nation's schools required a new "pro-American" curriculum. The report argues that "distorted histories" of the United States "labor under the illusion that slavery was somehow a uniquely American evil" and that the institution must "be seen in a much broader perspective," including "the unfortunate fact" that slavery "has been more the rule than the exception throughout human history." The document asserts that the civil rights movement evolved into "identity politics" when it said, "teaches America to blame itself for oppression."

If you are a white supremacist, this is the intellectual document for your followers. A complete history that they can embrace.

It also said that progressives had created a "fourth branch of government" or "shadow government" which operated with no checks or balances and likened American liberals to the Italian fascist leader Benito Mussolini, who it said, "sought to centralize power under the management of so-called experts." This *misinformation and misdirection* are key to successful fascists. Remember, always point the finger at your enemies to accuse them of being or doing exactly what you yourself are or are doing. Trump did it and reversed decades of civil rights for minorities and women. Blacks - unarmed or in their own beds - are now routinely shot by police with little repercussion.

Often on video.

American Klansmen

Commonly shortened to the KKK or the Klan, it is a homegrown American version of fascism. It began as a white supremacist hate group in response to northern liberal socialist thefts and carpet bagging. The primary targets are African Americans. Lesser enemies of the Klan include enabling Jews, immigrants, leftists, homosexuals, Muslims, and, intermittently, Catholics. The Klan has existed in three distinct eras at different points in time during the history of the United States. Each has advocated extremist reactionary positions such as white nationalism and anti-immigration.

The first Klan was established in the wake of the Civil War and was organized primarily in the Southern United States. It sought to overthrow the Republican state governments in the South, especially by using voter intimidation and targeted violence against African-American leaders. Each chapter was autonomous and highly secret as to membership and plans. Its numerous chapters across the South were suppressed around 1871 through federal law enforcement. Members made their own, often colorful, costumes: robes, masks, and conical hats, designed to be terrifying and to hide their identities. The second Klan started in Georgia in 1915 and employed marketing techniques and a popular fraternal organization structure rooted in local Protestant communities. This incarnation opposed Catholics and Jews while adding cross burnings and mass parades to intimidate others. It rapidly declined in the latter half of the 1920s (ref: Fred Trump training).

However, it was rabidly strong from 1890 - 1920. Racial and political murder were common.

The third and current manifestation of the KKK emerged after 1950 in the form of localized and isolated groups that use the KKK name. Supported by wealthy whites like Fred Trump, they had focused on opposition to the civil rights movement, often using violence and murder to suppress activists. Black men and women were being routinely hung by anonymous gangs of white-masked Klansmen who remained immune to prosecution by local authorities, their Klan brothers. The federal government, which has no law at the federal level for a local crime like murder, had to step in with federal troops and prosecute the murderers for the federal crime of 'deprivation of civil rights ("life, liberty, and pursuit of happiness").

Learning from previous and successful efforts to suppress the Klan, the 2016 and 2020 elections are notable for their strong Republican fascist content coupled with the absence of open Klan involvement, all the more surprising as the presidential candidate is the son of a Klan member and major financial contributor. Encouraged by the Republican 'tea party' extremists at the turn of the century, in retrospect, their strength in 2020 was predictable. They have changed tactics, and instead of standing outside the American political system or running within a party openly as Klansmen (ref: Gov. George Wallace), they have instead co-opted the existing political party, which most closely mirrored its own values (ala Sarah Palin). Doing so avoided uniting traditional Klan opposition and allowing new membership in their MAGA (Make America Great Again) movement without the older negative connotations.

Many paid attention to how far Palin – intellectually a political lightweight - got as a VP candidate.

The MAGA idea and phrase were lifted directly from the successful presidential campaigns of Ronald Reagan, who ironically, in his time, strongly opposed fascism. After the Palin presidential campaign of 2008, a revival of these ideas in the Tea Party galvanized a new generation and began the inevitable return to fascism in America. It made Trump's 2016 victory possible, slim a victory as that was in losing the popular vote but winning the electoral vote with the disinformation assistance of communist dictator Vladimir Putin and a general distrust of women in politics even by women (his opponent was a woman).

American Nazi Party

Neo-Nazism consists of post-World War II militant, social, or political movements seeking to revive and implement the ideology of Nazism. Neo-Nazis seek to employ their ideology to promote hatred and attack racial and ethnic minorities, promote white supremacy, or in some cases, create a separate fascist state. While many of the tenants of Nazism and specifically the American version, the recent WWII history of fighting versus German Nazi forces diminished the ability of the movement to be embraced by a significant percentage of fascist Americans until that generation grew old and died.

Most variations embrace a 14-word slogan, "We must secure the existence of our people and a future for white children," followed by the less commonly used "Because the beauty of the White Aryan woman must not perish from the Earth."

It has continued to appeal to young males and provides a source of violent members who can be recruited by more mature fascist movements, like the Qanon & Proud Boy branches of the Republican party. This technique continues to be employed by national organizations recruiting operatives from fragmented local Klan groups and cells. In another effort to disguise their Nazi roots, the fascist group known as Proud Boys openly oppose anti-fascist sentiments and protesters, drinking in public and refusing to wear masks during the corona pandemic. Biker groups & Qanon members often make common cause with fascists for their disdain of measures to control them and their misogynist & racial tenants.

On the front lines for any fascist leader are the numerous individually run militias scattered around a country. Humans are what they are, and in every nation, a significant percentage of men feel the same way: they embrace certain militaristic ideas in camaraderie to oppose what they see as liberals giving away welfare and preferential treatment to anyone but them. They are ripe for recruitment, and the beauty is *you can encourage them without explicitly* calling for illegal acts or violence. They will hear you and act on their own using your keywords, allowing you to distance yourself from unsuccessful carnage but take credit for victories. Just as police know that 9 of 10 times they shoot an unarmed suspect to death, they will not only be free men but likely continue to be police officers. A little word of encouragement from a President to militias will confirm they are acting patriotic when committing arson, murder, vote to block, intimidation of the President's enemies, and successfully acting as unpaid front-line troops. Brown shirts without the shirts.

The January 6th storming of the Congress resulted in *hundreds* of arrests, but *thousands* of new recruits arrived. They now visibly intimidate cowardly politicians, school boards, and election officials. Even librarians (seeking the hearts & minds of the young) are under assault.

Government Eugenics Program

Eugenics has been described as a scientific organized practice that aims to improve the genetic quality of a human population, historically by excluding people and groups judged to be inferior or promoting those judged to be superior. Human farmers and ranchers have used these techniques for millennia, resulting in cows with udders of unnatural size, more meat on poultry and beef cattle, and improved strains of grain with more edible food content & improved resistance to insects or disease.

It works. Evolution is a fact. Ask any farmer or rancher. Just don't use the E-word around religious supporters.

Targets of the eugenics movement were those who were seen as unfit for society—the poor, the disabled, the mentally ill, etc. A disproportionate number of those who fell victim to eugenicist sterilization initiatives were women who identified as African American, Hispanic, or Native American. While ostensibly about improving genetic quality, clearly, eugenics was more about preserving the position of the dominant white groups in the population. American efforts actually became an inspiration for German programs. This is effective and is a tool of fascism not to be overlooked by a strong enough leader.

In the guise of humanitarian and scientific improvement, one can hinder future generations of groups who, by their very nature, are least able to defend themselves. It is often a win for the species but always a win for those in power. The annihilation of European Hebrews by Nazi Germany was less about improving the species (which was always the spoken rationale) than about wealth redistribution from Jews who were smarter in business than most non-Judaic counterparts. The choice of that group - who largely kept to themselves due to religious principles - was brilliant. It decimated potential political opposition and rewarded non-intellectual rank-and-file supporters. In America, Jews are only 2% of the population.

So what if it actually weakened the country's intellectual pool?

The 1927 case of Buck v. Bell is infamous for Justice Oliver Wendell Holmes's thundering conclusion: "Three generations of imbeciles are enough." By a vote of 8 to 1, the Supreme Court of the U.S. allowed the forced sterilization of Carrie Buck by the state of Virginia. Buck's was the first of thousands of such sterilizations in the state before the practice was ended in 1974. Virginia's stated intent was to prevent Buck, already a single mother, and the others from conceiving "genetically inferior" children. It was effectively used against poor blacks and others.

Buck v. Bell was a great legal victory for the American eugenics movement, which, via a misunderstanding of genetics, strove to perfect the "race" and "white" civilization. The pseudo-science of eugenics emerged in the 1890s. It was a Progressive Era cause with the financial backing of the Carnegie Foundation, John D. Rockefeller, Fred Trump, and other fascist plutocrats. A true scientific program would be based much as farmers base theirs. Instead, it was and can be again successfully employed against politically undesirable individuals.

Even after the discrediting of the American government-supported effort, it continued to be used sporadically by fascists as a form of policy against specific groups deemed undesirable, in inner cities against Negroes and on a large scale versus native American Indians. Reports of forced sterilization of native American women began to surface in the 1970s. Of the 100,000 to 150,000 women of child-bearing age, 3,400 to 70,000 of these women were involuntarily sterilized through tubal ligation or hysterectomy. They were not given a choice to refuse or accept to undergo the sterilization procedure. The diminished numbers of natives on reservations today, with diminished economic strength in competition with whites, is due in no small part to the success of these efforts.

Repeat them when you can.

A counter anti-abortion argument can be made that allowing poor blacks and immigrants to breed like flies is an effective way to keep them all poor. If allowed to vote, however, this can become disastrous.

Police Forces

Much as religious institutions whose shamans or priests are forbidden to marry, thus inviting homosexuals and child predators, the nature of a police force in physically enforcing laws and public policy by force of arms, beatings, imprisonment, or even death attracts a specific type of individual. Much is made in advertising and marketing the policeman as a friend of the neighborhood and a trusted authority figure in times of trouble, but the reality is far different. Power corrupts, and the ability to kill with almost total impunity attracts sadistic individuals. Though most policemen spend an entire career without killing, the lesser uses of force and coercion are very appealing to this minority of effective staff you wish to recruit.

Those types of individuals have always been used to implement political policy. In third-world countries, secret police forces who wear masks and only report to commanders at the top are prevalent. They are even more feared than the public police force. President Trump himself used and defended this practice during the race riots in Portland, Oregon.

In America, the police forces in large cities developed in the 1800s into bully squads that controlled their districts with rapid violence far in excessive proportion to the threats faced. In small towns and villages, the local lawman and his deputies *to this day* are often minor dictators in their own right and can act with almost total impunity. Intimidation thru rape, physical domination, and support by powerful industrial or wealthy persons make them untouchable. In President Trump's own time before becoming president, his purchase of the Helmsley Palace Hotel in NYC was rapidly followed by the sudden disappearance of homeless beggars in the area, as his nameless enforcers grabbed them, transported them to slum areas, and beat them unconscious - the lesson was soon learned, and his high priced hotel was free of the usual NYC neighborhood beggars. I lived in NYC at the time.

Opportunities arise from opposition to this (apparent) negative image. One only needs to look at the recent civil rights movement ('black lives matter') to see their gift to fascism in the form of their one common action item: *de-fund the police*. People who were wavering in your support suddenly and clearly had an enemy they could focus upon. Could understand. The idea of de-funding the police was antithetical to decent, law-abiding white citizens tired of being smugly lectured to by welfare families and liberal-socialist intellectuals. It became real. A critical mistake by your enemies.

America in Wartime

Never let the opposition give you doubts about the utility of your positions. When push comes to shove, people always turn to violence to solve their problems. Using the example of America once more, consider American actions during wartime. Suspension of 'inalienable rights' is common and almost automatic. Search and seizure within the homes of citizens is suddenly justified. Interring citizens who have committed no crimes or aggressions against the country in concentration camps (Japanese in the 1940s) becomes policy. Protest is met with violence or imprisonment. Those unwilling to volunteer for the war are drafted into it (President Johnson saw to it that mostly black or poor went to Vietnam though officers were white), and imprisoned if caught fleeing. Free enterprise to choose what you manufacture or where you work during wartime is dictated by the government anywhere they have a need.

These are all part of American history, and at the time they were instituted were considered *patriotic acts* for the benefit of the nation.

If your enemies say you are acting in an un-American manner or improperly under the law, remind them what they themselves, and the country as a whole have always done. Europeans did not 'discover' and bring people to the Americas - people were already here until European pirates came, stole their lands, and murdered them. We went from 13 east coast colonies to expanding into western territories where we slaughtered millions of native opposition, broke every treaty we ever made, and herded survivors onto otherwise useless lands unless, of course, minerals or water rights were later found there. A true fascist acts just like the Romans, giving undeveloped border lands to invading Goths, Visigoths, and Huns to provide a bulk ward against other barbarian tribes but never allowing them full or any rights of citizenship within the empire.

Support and defend the constitution as the highest law of the land, for like all Bibles and the best of central government documents, you can do whatever you like within it if you are strong enough to push for it. If the bleeding hearts of later generations condemn the actions, see if they are willing to give back most of the country to surviving native tribes. Watch how fast they shut up. Let them talk and empathize all they want as long as it does not interfere with your policies or profits, or power.

US History:

1. During the late 20th and early 21st century, Arab opposition suspects or others believed to have information on opposition groups - though not at war with their governments, nor were they our own citizens - were imprisoned. This is illegal on American soil, so the government used Guantanamo Bay military base in Cuba to evade the legal requirement for counsel, trial, and prohibition of torture. Other countries as well.
2. Until 1974, the US Government had a policy of sterilization for misfits, undesirables, those with hereditary diseases, etc. This policy was only enforced on the poor or political enemies.
3. During WWII, Japanese American citizens were rounded up and placed in concentration camps in California, the closest state to a potential Japanese invasion. They had committed no crimes.
4. One lesson amid dozens about fairness exemplifies native American slaughter. The Cherokee Indian tribe of the east coast Carolinas were forcibly removed to empty Oklahoma, traveling largely on foot. Most died. Upon finding oil in Oklahoma, treaties ceding those lands to them were dissolved, and they were again pushed onto more useless lands by white Christian

authorities. This was in the best interest of an expanding white population.

5. In the defense of New Orleans during the Spanish-American war, criminals and pirates were promised amnesty for all crimes and full citizenship or reinstatement of rights. Once the close battle was won with their aid, they were driven from the city. Many were arrested and hung or shot as an example to the others.

6. One of the criticisms of Germany under Nazi rule was their use of slave factory labor and imprisonment of ethnic groups when they used those methods to rise from the ruin of WWI to efficiently control all of mainland Europe. Americans neglected the fact we did the same thing when building our nation after fighting a guerilla war of liberation from Great Britain, including generations of slave labor from Africa in agriculture and indentured white labor in factories. In founding the country, slavery was not prohibited. And after the slave-freeing civil war, industrialization grew using indentured serfs.

7. One of the criticisms of Arab governments was the suppression of citizen rights and the killing of civilians in opposition to your rule. Yet we bombed civilian populations in target cities from Germany to Vietnam when they opposed our policies. When Germany was defeated, we did not 'free' Arab territories under German control, but switched that control to ourselves,

Great Britain, and France for the oil therein. Our Russian allies similarly focused on controlling the countries east of Germany for their mineral deposits, agriculture, and labor force.

8. Citizens of New York State in the 1960s were presented with a referendum to allow or prohibit capital punishment for the crime of murder. The opposition presented the fact that of convicted murderers, 1 in 10 were eventually found to be innocent and should not be killed. The proponents presented the fact that if convicted of murder, 8 of 10 felons were known to commit another murder within 10 years. Result: voters chose to allow 8 innocent people to die at someone else hands rather than kill one innocent on their own. The average man is your cattle. As one who would lead them, remember this.

9. While citizens are supposed to have 'inalienable rights,' with the right of property ownership among the strongest of them, the government can and has forced citizens to 'sell' their property when the government wants it, for a price set by the government below actual value, whether they want to sell or not. It is called 'eminent domain.'

10. In the great liberal push for civil rights in the 1960s, leftist politicians pushed for and created 'affirmative action' programs to give blacks and other minorities preferential treatment in getting housing, university admissions, and jobs.

This violated the rights of hard-working non-minorities who competed for the same housing, educational opportunities, and jobs. Unknown until decades later, one of the largest financial supporters of the program through campaign donations to these leftist politicians was the Ku Klux Klan. They realized it would result in generations of minority children growing up *knowing they were not good enough* to compete with whites. Similarly, they supported non-English language classes in schools, which resulted in many minority students never fully mastering English and placing them at a disadvantage in the workplace. It was and is felt one of the best ways to *'keep minorities down.'*

And would make fresh generations of young whites angry at blacks for getting a free ride. And encourage minority children not to learn. To this day, their reading scores are abysmal.

11. Realizing that giving every citizen a vote in the presidential election would never favor fascists or small states, the founders of America instituted a program whereby citizens vote for a number of 'electors,' who themselves vote for the President. By tradition, they vote for whoever won the popular vote in their state, but it is specifically not required. In addition, several times in the last 50 years, the person winning the popular vote nationwide lost, just as the system was designed to achieve.

12. Realizing the average person is unintelligent, a follower, and violent if repressed long enough, they were given the appearance of democracy by the founders of America in a legislative chamber of Representatives based on population. By correctly drawing congressional 'district' lines breaking up concentrations of minorities, their voting can be diluted and overcome (gerrymandering). In addition, a second chamber of Congress, the Senate, was created with only 2 members per state. No law could be made by Congress unless *both* chambers agree on it. The result was that aristocratic control could be maintained while giving the appearance of a democracy. This is called a republic. For example, the two Senators from California & New York could be outvoted by senators from 6 or 7 states with small populations, even though combined, they represented far fewer people by a lot. This is American 'democracy' today.
13. Reacting to unfriendly foreign governments, several American leaders embraced fascist methods to have them assassinated or foment revolution in those countries, thus weakening a perceived or potential enemy.

    The ones below had democratically elected governments:

1973 Chile - under Nixon installed an army Junta

1964 Brazil - under Kennedy ordered a military coup

1960 Congo - the assassination of Lumumba and installed Colonel Mobutu

1954 Guatemala - installed dictator Armas

1953 Iran - installed dictator The Shah

1949 Syria - installed military dictator Colonel Za'im

1941 Panama - entered a civil war & got military bases

The ones below attempted a democratically elected government.

2019 Syria – under Trump, withdrew troops supporting democratic rebels allowing their

slaughter by Putin's Russian troops & aided Turkey in repressing the Kurds.

2014 Ukraine - democratically elected president was overthrown by a USA coup.

2011 Egypt – (we abandoned their Arab Spring)

1968 Czechoslovakia – (Prague Spring supporters slaughtered)

... and many more!

The 21ˢᵗ Century

For those who mistakenly believe these are all actions of the past, they cannot embrace in today's media-rich environment, think again. You can and should.

For example, a trend began in 2018 to reinstitute slavery. That's right, slavery, and it barely made a ripple in the media.

Five states had slavery on the ballot in 2022. Alabama, Louisiana, Vermont, Oregon, and Tennessee voted in November to remove language in their state constitutions that allow those convicted of a crime to be punished with slavery and indentured servitude. Well known is most prisoners are black or Hispanic, well out of proportion to their national population.

Colorado, Nebraska, and Utah have already passed similar laws scrubbing slavery from the books–a trend that didn't start until 2018. Just as most non-Jews state openly that Nazi Germany could never happen in America, slavery is making a big comeback. It is the ultimate expression of the will to power: to effectively not just incarcerate those who violate your rules but to own them.

The US military overseas, our bastion fighting for freedom, is just as guilty. Thousands of people are today trafficked into labor by private contractors on U.S. military bases — where workers have been paid less than promised, charged recruiting fees that leave them deep in debt and pressured to sign improper contracts and work long hours, according to government reports. They even face physical abuse. No one dares speak for them or else be accused of being against our military.

Remember, too, that it has long been held by the federal prison system that inmates can be forced to work, some being paid $0.52/hr (the legal minimum wage is over $10/hr), and in some states, there is no payment at all.

Nothing is off the table. Wake up and embrace the power that comes from taking and using power.

Chapter 3

PRINCIPLES OF FASCISM

1. A good leader displays strength thru intimidation
    1.1 A strong leader does not tolerate opposing viewpoints.
    1.2 A strong leader makes quick decisions and sticks with them, even when proven incorrect.
    1.3 A strong leader is not told what to believe - he tells people what to believe
2. A good follower is an obedient follower

    2.1 A good follower believes what the leader tells him
    2.2 A good follower does not contradict the leader even when you know he is wrong
    2.3 A good follower will repeat what the leader says as the unquestioned truth

Late in 2022 for the congressional elections, armed right-wing Republicans began showing up at polling places. They took photos, recorded license plates, and brandished assault weapons. A Trump-appointed court ruled armed men in fatigues at ballot boxes aren't intimidating voters. Wow. With this encouragement, imagine what they will do in the 2024 election!

Learn the lesson: you can go farther than you think. And your followers will go even farther.

3. Anyone who opposes you opposes what is right for the nation

3.1 Opponents of the leader are traitors to the nation

3.2 Opponents of the leader are always incorrect, even when you know they are not

3.3 Opponents of the leader opposed what the nation was founded upon, even when they do not

3.4 Binary thinking: any success for your opponents hurts your followers

For example, GOP officials, sword to uphold the law, refused to follow the law and accept subpoenas to testify about what they saw & knew after the January 6th insurrection.

In another example, Trump attacked Biden & DeSantis, touring hurricane damage as fake news. Concerning binary thinking, anything which is a success to your opponents – even if it is a good thing for the country as a whole – can somehow be painted as a bad thing for your supporters.

-Limiting automatic weapons used in slaughtering children in schools = they are treading on your right to bear arms.

- Extending the right to vote to former black slaves and other minorities = dilutes your vote.

4. The national good is more important than the individual good (except your own good leadership)

   4.1 Followers must sacrifice for the greater good

   4.2 What the leader says is for the national good is, by definition, the national good

   Soldiers go where they are told and kill who they are told.

   Disobeying police or fighting back when they murder unarmed civilians is unpatriotic.

   Donate money to our campaigns, and we shall protect you from the enemy.

   Doctors, nurses, meat packers, and others working risky occupations during a pandemic without protective equipment should shut up and get back to work.

   A leader does not have to have a military background to lead the military and to make military decisions not agreed with by military professionals. Neither does he have to be a successful businessman to lead the economy and to make economic decisions not agreed with by business professionals. Trump may have lost multiple casinos due to mismanagement, and his university was a dismal failure, but supporters will ignore these things. A leader does not have to be a medical expert to control the healthcare system and to make decisions not agreed with by medical professionals. Feel free to attack the opinions of professionals who have spent their entire careers in one area, usually by attacking them personally.

5. A regimented economy benefits everyone (especially leadership).

5.1 Regimentation does not mean excessive regulations if they interfere with profits

5.2 Lack of regulations allows corporate entities to thrive at the expense of employees, customers, and the environment

5.3 Everyone participates in a wartime economy. Declare the need for wartime regulation whenever there is resistance or illegality to any desired action

6. All nations look out for their own best interest.

6.1 Protectionism and tariffs are preferred to open trade

6.2 Just as with people, strong nations always dominate weak nations

6.3 Pressure can be applied to get what you want at the international level by:

6.3a - actual or threatened military action

6.3b - economic pressure

6.3c - bribery or quid-pro-quo agreements

6.3d - international agreements can always be abandoned when your needs or circumstances change

7. Opponents of fascism based on differing core principles

Liberalism - characterize them as trying to give away everything you work hard for or lazy criminals

Democracy - the illusion that a large number of men know better than a single dynamic leader is a great lie & used by your opponents to gain support from their cattle

Marxism -needlessly complex socioeconomic analysis & dialectic perspective designed to deceive freedom-loving people into bowing to an underclass of lesser peoples

Anarchism -embraced by the lawless & anti-police to openly take what you have by force and violence

8. Allies of fascism include those with a shared desire for power at any cost

Dictators - characterized by strong central control, law, and order, suppression of civil protests, and control of the media

Kings -see dictators

Military Junta - dictatorship by military committee

Hereditary Monarchy - dictatorship by family members of an original dynamic leader

9. Daily fascist techniques of rule and intimidation: do at least one every day

9.1 Accuse your opposition of doing exactly what you yourself are doing

9.2 Accuse your accuser or opponent of being stupid or incompetent

9.3 Arrest your political opponents without cause

9.4 Smear your opponent with unfounded accusations

>(put words they never said in their mouth, then rebut them)

9.5 Threaten attack or have followers physically assault opponents

9.6 Discredit investigative media so they will not be believed

9.7 Have your own outlets for disinformation

9.8 Invent an unseen dangerous enemy against which to attack

9.9 Frighten the public with imaginary disasters to sow discontent if you are ever replaced

9.10 Share inside information with supporters or potential supporters (the greedy will see gain)

9.11 Hide past records of your actual actions & beliefs

9.12 A secret police force will inspire fear and encourage violence from lack of accountability

9.13 Prevent or hinder opposition voices from being heard

9.14 Prevent or hinder opposition votes from being counted

9.15 Create loyalty lists to inspire loyalty and enemies list to inspire intimidation

10. If you cannot win an election, steal an election.

    10.1 Elections have been stolen in the past two centuries through a variety of mechanisms.

    Some allow the public to believe they elected the winner. Others, like a dictator declaring that only he can vote and then votes for himself, are clearly not the will of the public, though a true fascist leader will state he knows his people better than they do. Some of the more overt mechanisms have included rigged voting machines, payoffs to those counting the ballots, shutting polling places in opposition strongholds, controlling the post office, armed vigilantes at ballot boxes, and various other intimidation techniques to keep your opponents away from polling places.

    10.2 Peripheral violence can be incited

    In a nation with an apparent history of non-violent elections, as authorities will be unaccustomed to dealing with such methods. The phrase 'Nazi Germany could never happen here' was echoed again and again after World War II, with the small unheeded voices of surviving Hebrews insisting, 'Yes, it can!"

    10.3 Use the complexities of multiple state election laws to confuse and obfuscate your plans.

Begin - months ahead of the election – by insisting that your opponents plan to commit massive fraud and steal the election. No evidence is needed, and it falls within the precept of accusing your opponents of what you yourself are doing to rile up your base and throw doubt onto your opponents' legitimacy when they win. This will ensure your political importance even after you lose. Next, also months before the election, inform your supporters not to vote by mail but vote in person. The reason becomes clear when you appoint a million-dollar donor to run the post office & limit and delay voting by mail, causing massive last-minute backups. In addition, you petition legislatures and local election officials not to allow the counting of mailed-in votes until election day. Then, as election day approaches, begin legal maneuvers and lawsuits to say any mailed-in votes not received by election day should not be counted. Then use that to say any mailed-in votes not counted by election day do not count, saying they must be fraudulent as they came out of nowhere, yet everyone knew where they came from: your own delaying actions. The final step is to force thru your judicial appointments to the court system, giving the courts a conservative-leaning, who, if enough states do not cave in to your pressure, intimidation, or bribery, will support your illegal actions. In an electoral system, begin by counting all the votes of legitimate voters. Then supportive governors of lost states will appoint your own slate of electors - ignoring the public vote - and the courts will back their treasonous coup.

10.4 Non-violent passive-aggressive techniques can be employed by supporters who would shy away from violence themselves.

For example, in the campaign of Michael Peroutka, the Republican candidate to be Maryland's attorney general, Peroutka campaign manager Mackey Stafford was caught on video encouraging supporters to show up late to polling places to create long lines that could potentially discourage Democratic voters from casting their ballots. Illegal but effective without overt violence. Clever.

10.5 Military Action

A well-thought-out and well-orchestrated campaign taking months, as described above, nearly succeeded in an astonished 2020 America. That left only overt military action, whether taking over voting stations in specific states to the assassination of state opposition leaders & intimidation of election officials, such as the attempt to kill Governor Whitman & House Speaker Pelosi. As these were just tests for 2024, data was collected, and preparations must be made based on how far we now know your followers can be pushed.

In 2020, the US military was – overall - not ready to commit treason. Magas were.

The opposition liberals are not immune to violent followers, such as the Scalese shooting and the attack on Rand Paul, but it is not a policy with them and, therefore, not effective. Paint your opposition with the same violent extremist brush. In truth, private citizen violence is a necessary preparation for a coup. It identifies those who will stand with you when push comes to shove and mobilizes citizen support while intimidating your opponents.

11. If you cannot steal the election, secede from the nation to form your own

11.1 With enough support from the populace or disenchantment with an existing government, you can form your own. As with America from Britain, a majority is not required. A flood of like-minded believers has recently flooded mountain states with low populations. Texas began as another country.

11.2 You must have your supporters willing to do what the opposition will not.

No nation on the face of the Earth today has been there from the beginning of recorded history. Some were formed by armed revolt against a distant foreign power. Others formed by an armed revolt in civil war against an existing government. Occasionally it is transitioned peacefully, as when colonial powers granted independence to certain colonies in the 19th and 20th centuries. Peaceful transition is rare. Occasionally, civil warfare is so violent and destructive, such as in Czechoslovakia, that other countries join in to appoint their own government or support one or more sides outright with financial aid or military troops. When the foreign overlord USSR withdrew from eastern Europe territories, war erupted. There are now three countries in the ruins of where Czechoslovakia once stood. Removal of fascist authority under the Soviet Union *was a disaster* for civilians.

A splendid example is provided by the American Trump campaign in 2020, where after losing the final electoral case at the Supreme Court, a call was made by Republicans in Texas to secede from the union. This was not made by fringe militias and thugs but by several in party leadership.

A cult gaining momentum in 2022 is flooding the Montana & Dakota areas with supporters of religious succession. Locals were outraged but helpless given the rules for 'civil' and 'polite' behavior they themselves have sworn to obey. New religious movements founded in the region include: The Cascadia movement promotes the idea of a bioregion covering the watersheds of the Columbia, Fraser, and Snake rivers. The State of Jefferson and many others are alive and well, with violent extremist followers. If you are publically friendly towards them – even without condoning succession like talks in Texas – you will get their votes as the only mainstream candidate who dares do so.

12 .Your Movement Loses.

Whether it is an election or just getting masses of people motivated to act for you, with violence when necessary, there are times when you will lose. When Texas lost to Mexico in their attempt to hold the land they stole. When slavery in America was overthrown when the southern states - forming their own country called The Confederacy - lost to the northern states in the original Union. When the Klu Klux Klan failed in the 1920s to secure control of the federal government (but came close).

Though you know when you are beaten, never admit defeat. Never acknowledge a loss. Every time a fascist movement or leader acknowledges their loss, they are truly lost. It then takes years if not generations to climb back into power. Look at the American examples above. Remember to always be a sore loser. There is no prize for second best in the domination of a nation or a people. Leave being a good sport to your opposition.

And when defeated, immediately begin attacking the winner(s). Look for an example in the Confederacy, throwing sand into the gears of reconstruction. In Hitler's Germany, a nation after being beaten and humiliated under the Kaiser in WWI, climbed back within a few short years to be within a hair's breadth of being in control of the Earth via the axis powers (Germany, Italy & Japan).

Fascism is efficient. Fascism works and has the most motivated followers of any political persuasion. The dispassionate, intellectual liberals of America are finding that out the hard way.

Look at how the Nazi rhetoric focused on the humiliation Germany was suffering under the peace accord after WWI. Stirring up patriotism. Giving a focus for hatred of the life being led by losers, who may even have been losers before the war and still were. Give them focus & an enemy to hate. With every victory, verbal or material, over the conditions of the WWI peace treaty, with every move and appeasement by your enemies as you march from one country to another, your enemies will be more respectful & fearful of you overseas. Your own people will be encouraged and believe in your strength & unsupported opinions all the more.

Never admit you lost. You were cheated. Robbed. And you had the strength to take it back. This will encourage your existing supporters, gather new supporters, and confuse or frighten those who will never support you anyway. Remember, your rhetoric is *not directed at converting the left*.

13. Strange Bedfellows

13.1 Your followers have natural enemies – discredit and attack them at every opportunity.

13.2 Surprise the enemy by embracing a class of people they thought they could count upon.

A leader cannot focus on the day to day working of a government. That is not his job, whether a fascist, king, monarch, elected president or minister. It is the job of clerks and bureaucrats. The job of a leader is to set the tone using the principles above.

A prime example was the Hebrew population of 20th-century Germany. Too educated to relate to by the majority of simpler folk. Living standards higher than average with that higher than average education and work ethic. Private community with traditions that differ from the majority. And too small in population to effectively oppose you. In the current situation, the surprisingly effective motivation of the voter base is made by weaponizing the jealousy and distrust of American Jews. Need we say more?

In terms of a surprise to the enemy, this pair of recent well-organized and brilliant moves, both the Hispanic and negro communities have been effectively invaded by right-wing propaganda. The liberals counted on both communities and were slack in actually doing anything to actually improve their lives.

Thinking wall-building white supremacists could not possibly appeal to Hispanics and blacks, the left was caught flat-footed by several Hispanic and black candidates openly embraced and promoted by the right. No matter their qualifications. No matter their record of public sins and lack of public service. In fact, they were embraced by their kind because of their flaws! Ever so clever, and after three years of application bearing real fruit to the dismay of progressive party leaders. And of old-school Republicans.

Chapter 4

EVENTS A FASCIST LEADER WILL ENCOUNTER

The following events cannot be avoided. At some time, if you are successful enough and climb the rungs of power high enough, they will certainly occur. Do not let them dismay you. See them as *opportunities to display your strength* and crush opposition. In this next section, we shall detail true events for each and how to respond to them.

E1. Caught lying or being wrong
Deny all evidence. Never admit being wrong. Never admit even an obvious lie. Never apologize.

Shortly before the 2022 congressional elections, Conservative frustration with fact-checkers continued to grow after several PolitiFact articles pointed out falsehoods or outright lies by conservatives. While this sparked outrage from media critics and right-leaning Twitter users, the leaders have two clear pathways to deal with such things.

1. Acknowledge you were misinformed, misspoke, or in some way unintentionally said what you said.
2. Ignore being caught and plow ahead.
3. Attack those who caught you as:
   -being politically biased
   -doing exactly what you did
   -accuse your accuser of being stupid or incompetent

The weak generally chose option (a). The stubbornly belligerent often chose option (b). The intelligent leader combines (b) with (c), knowing that by confronting being caught, you will place reasonable doubt in the minds of your followers. Remember, the opposition will never believe you anyway, so by option (c) you are turning a negative into a positive by showing your strength and determination to supporters.

E2. Political opponents are more popular

Attack them ruthlessly. Disparage their reputation. Create evidence or simply insist, with emotional fervor, that they are not what they seem.

That they are guilty. And then jump to their just punishment. If not them, their families or staff.

An election is held. You lose. You complain and insist it was stolen, but the truth is the truth: the majority of the population doesn't want you. You can still retain power once in office by the oldest tactic in the book: declaring martial law. It allows you to mobilize armed troops to suppress the will of the people. In a republic like America, Article V of the constitution allows modification of that constitution without the approval of Congress. It can legitimize the declaration of martial law.

Study the weak 'January 6 Insurrection'. This was not a serious attempt but a dry run to gauge response. Former Trump administration Homeland Security official Miles Taylor said he believes the former president wanted members of Congress to be killed on January 6. The President was forcibly restrained from joining the attack by the Secret Service. Taylor describes himself as part of a "resistance" within the executive branch. He argued the former president would have used such deaths as a pretext to declare martial law and remain in office in perpetuity.

About 4 in 10 fascist leaders have gained or retained power by this simple expedient. History repeats.

E3. The public rises against you

Deny the majority opposes you. Paint the opposition as criminals doing exactly what you yourself are doing.

Label those who rise against you as terrorists or whatever term is suitable in that decade or century. Enable your Gestapo police and military and federal agents (secret police) to commit the most violent atrocities against them in the name of justice. And if one of your people is attacked, *paint all the opposition* as violent criminals.

Truck drivers form a convoy and circle the White House to protest his ignoring Covid protections and endangering them. Trump said on camera the drivers loved him and were showing their support. Maintain that positive spin on the most obvious contrary event.

Nurses invited to the White House in the worst days of Covid-19 surrounded the President as he spoke of giving them his full support and plenty of protective equipment. A senior nurse dared to interrupt him and state clearly on camera how they were here today to get that level of support commitment because they were out of everything and re-using masks & gloves! The President took control, interrupted her, and stated flat out, "That is not my information. I made sure you have everything you need, don't you?" She cowered and agreed in a low, embarrassed voice. The other 15 nurses said nothing, shifting uncomfortably in their standing positions.

E4. Established leaders or the judicial system rise up against you.

Label them enemies of the nation. Choose a traditional target group or political movement whom the public hates or views automatically as the enemy, and label your opponent as that. Also, labor them as traitors to your nationalistic movement if they at one time supported or appeared to support you.

Another technique, one employed effectively by Trump, is intimidation of the judiciary. With the evidence against him in the Trump University fraud case, rather than deferring to his lawyers or reserving his rhetoric against students behind the class-action lawsuit, Trump impugned the character of the federal judge presiding over the case. "I have a judge who is a hater of Donald Trump, a hater. He's a hater," Trump said of Judge Gonzalo Curiel. The future president noted the Indiana-born judge's Mexican heritage to question whether he could rule impartially in the Trump University case, as Trump advocated building a wall with Mexico.

How do his followers implement & give backbone to such attacks?

-At least three packages with white powder arrived at the federal courthouse in Washington, DC.

-Federal judges involved in matters related to the FBI's search of Mar-a-Lago also faced threats.

-The number of logged threats to judges and other officials doubled early in the Trump era.

The remarks set the tone for what legal experts saw as Trump's politicization of the federal judiciary. Trump would go on to win the election, and his four-year White House term would coincide with a remarkable rise in threats to federal judges and other officials under the protection of the US Marshals Service.

E5. Personal enrichment opportunities

A traditional method for political self-enrichment comes from the sharing (or withholding) of inside information. Like military contracts. Covid was expected to trash the stock market, so while telling the public covid would be over in a month, Trump wisely told Republican senators the truth & they made a fortune as the equities market collapsed. He continued to manipulate Covid-19 information for profit as Americans died. When what you claim is proven wrong (it was), say you were misled by others (blame Dr. Fauci). Remember the factual sequence.

January-February 2020 received information from the Chinese and the World health Organization that a highly infectious, lethal virus had not been contained.

February 2020 - meeting at the White House with Republican senators & congressmen to tell them the virus effect will be severe and require a temporary shutdown of businesses &

travel; senators sell stock holdings and short the market.

February 2020 - Publicly state the virus is no problem. It is contained and will be gone in 15 days, Easter at the latest.

March 2020 - announce that the virus effect will be severe and require a temporary shutdown of businesses & travel; stock market tumbles & fortunes are made by warned insiders; the public lost fortunes.

July 2020 - award a $300 million grant to Kodak Corporation to switch from photography to making anti-viral chemicals for pharmaceutical companies; inform White House loyalists and family to use off shore accounts; stock triples two days before a public announcement is made. In a two-headed win, Trump accuses Democrats of fixing the election results while rewarding political donors. Trump appointed a new head of the US Postal Service who never worked there; the man owns competing businesses: no more Saturday delivery, election ballots no longer first class mail, shut down mail sorting machines, eliminate overtime during heavy voting season. His appointed head of the post office donated a cool $1 million to Trump's campaign. And even better, Trump himself commented on slowing down mailing votes (largely democratic), "If every citizen voted, there would never be another Republican elected in this country."

A second main perk is to protect yourself from criminal liability even when discovered or removed from office. The use of Presidential pardons for yourself, your family, and key supporters will prevent them from turning on you if they have been arrested or convicted themselves. Your get-out-of-jail-free card should be played heavily as needed. Many believe he is only running in 2024 to shield himself from democratic attacks.

Rep. Jim Banks (R-IN) hired Carlson's son, Buckley Carlson, as one of his staffers because the Indiana congressman wanted to please the GOP establishment and therefore boost his chances of becoming House majority whip if Republicans take back the chamber. Carlson called National Republican Congressional Committee Chair Rep. Tom Emmer (R-MN), who's competing with Banks over the coveted leadership slot, and demanded that he find out which staff member made that comment,

"He hires Tucker Carlson's son, a 24-year-old kid, to be his communications director."

Carlson was clearly not upset about his kid being hired for a position he did not deserve, and it's a perk of being a propaganda media host for his party. He rightly was furious that someone spoke the truth to the media. That person was subsequently found and severely punished. Lesson learned that loose lips sink ships.

E6. Military Service (not for you - this is for the cattle)

While publicly extolling the virtues of those who wear a uniform (police & military), understand this is not for you or yours. This is for fools who place themselves in the line of fire.

Never place yourself in the line of fire just to get credentials like JF Kennedy or George Bush.

E7. Requirement for Credentials

Lie or bribe those in positions to support your claims of credentials or achievements whenever possible. The more outrageous and unlikely the claim (an Ivy League degree, a genius IQ), the more it will be believed by the weak-minded masses. Look at Herschel Walker.

Military service is often a plus for presidential candidates. Do not simply avoid service, but have a 'medical excuse.'

Tactic: Trump was diagnosed as a young man just before being drafted by a pediatrician in a low-rent neighborhood. His landlord was Trump's father. Enemies will question why a rich boy like him went to a discount doctor. So? Believers want to believe.

Intelligence is often looked upon as a credential in a leader, as is a college degree.

Tactics: Purchase admission to a college. If

difficult, purchase term papers. Hide your transcripts which show you are dull-witted intellectually. Refuse to take IQ tests. For those who have intimate knowledge of your crime because they are doing the same thing, pardon them in the last month in office: a Miami developer was accused of securing his daughter's admission to USC through bribery and fraud.

A Presidential debate is often an opportunity to show how quick-witted or intelligent you are. It will also showcase how mentally dull you are compared to an intelligent opponent. Three were scheduled between Trump and Biden.

Tactic: Since you are intelligent but not intellectual, act as a bully by constantly interrupting the proceedings in a manner to reduce the event to a shouting match. Even if the opponent does not fall for it, you evade revealing you are just average or below average & may cause your opponent to lose his temper. Their debates were terminated after the second one, full of lies and off-topic misinformation. And praise from the MAGA media.

E8. Association with unpopular organizations or people

You will of necessity be in a position where certain of your supporters are disliked by the majority for their violence or closed-mindedness. Show them verbal support then they will act to frighten others into hesitation when they should be openly opposing you. Only the strongest of your opponents will do so and thereby identify themselves to you for personal attack.

Best friends in NY with Epstein, pedophile & jailbait procurer for the rich; attended multiple sex parties with him. Broadcast in NY on Don Imus radio show as saying, "Epstein is a swell guy, great to hang out and party with."

Tactic: Accuse democratic opponents and the hidden deep state of being involved with pedophilia. Employ Rule 9.1 to accuse your would-be accusers. Your followers will be confused and default to you. Your enemies will be taken-aback and react in a flustered way, shocked at your bald-faced lies, harming their credibility.

Tactic: In January 2021, after the Supreme Court in which he had appointed 3 of the 9 judges personally, yet they refused to throw out the electoral count and install him as President, he bizarrely claimed that Supreme Court Chief Justice John Roberts is a murderous pedophile. Not so bizarre – consistent punishment for opponents and traitors to his cause.

Trump's father and grandfather were not only major players but major donors to the KluKlux-Clan.

Tactic: Wanting his son to eventually run for office if the opportunity in a fractured Republican party presented itself, which it did after the advent of S. Palin's 'tea party' within the RNC, Donald trump was never allowed to join the KKK officially, nor similar organizations reflecting his father and grandfather's beliefs. Those records would eventually have surfaced.

Tactic: Whenever caught and accused of any association or activity which can be labeled 'fascist,' counter-attack by calling yourself a 'law and order' person and a 'patriot, with America and American values first.'

E9. A law is passed limiting you, or you lose an election

Re-interpret the law to your own liking. Ignore it when it is clearly against you. Modify it to suit your own purposes. Study how a bible for Christianity which has as one of its central ten instructions from God himself, "Thou Shalt Not Kill," not only allows but commands the death of witches, heathens, blasphemers, etc., all the way up from individual murder to mass genocide in centuries of religious crusades. Anything can be twisted.

Trump fired Inspector Generals (IGs) and installed loyalists who would not interfere with or even investigate his tampering with legitimate operations of the government.

In April and May 2020, Trump dismissed the inspectors general (IGs) of five cabinet departments in the space of six weeks. The inspectors general removed were Michael K. Atkinson,

Intelligence, on April 3; Glenn Fine (acting), Defense, April 7; Christi Grimm (acting), Health and Human Services, May 1; Mitch Behm (acting), Transportation, May 15; and Steve Linick, State, May 15.

It was difficult to find people who would commit treason for so many posts, so at least a dozen of the 38 President appointed inspectors general will not be in place at the end of the Trump administration.

In late February, after acting DNI Joseph Maguire tasked a member of his staff to brief the House Intelligence Committee that the Russians were meddling in the 2020 election to re-elect Trump, he was out.

Trump nominated Brian Miller, who is currently serving as senior White House associate counsel, as Special Inspector General for pandemic recovery at the Treasury Department. Many such smart moves cement power by inhibiting government bureaucrats who might oppose you.

E10. A national disaster happens on your watch
If internationally linked, initially blame a foreign power. If completely domestic and limited to a geopolitical area, blame your opposition in that area for mismanagement. If truly national, claim it is not as bad as it seems and that every successful effort against it was by your hand personally. Trump minimizing Covid-19 severity as Americans die; says he has provided all the protective

equipment needed. Nurses meeting on camera with Trump at the White House stated they are reusing masks meant for a day for a full week & Trump says they are wrong and have plenty of PPE.

"That is not my information; you have plenty of PPE already." Consistency.

E11. Your power to officially act is limited

Take power you do not have - such as appointments - and force your opposition to act against you. If there are watchdog positions in government, such as various Inspectors General, fire them and install your own supporters. If blocked or repealed in your violations of law, circumvent opposition response completely by declaration of emergency or invoking martial law where you can suspend all previous laws.

Trump rewarded political supporter Pence with the vice presidency in exchange for evangelical and religious support. Pence named all the appointed conservative judges against their primary issue: abortion. Trump appointed 243 federal judges in 4 years. Obama appointed 56 in 8 years. Well done.

If the election becomes contested in the Supreme Court, appoint as many loyalist extremists to the court as you can. Trump appointed 3 Supreme Court justices in 4 years. Obama was blocked by the Republican senate from appointing more than 2 in 8 years. Anti-American? Well done I say.

E12. Position on foreign relations with allies
Allies are competitors in sheep's clothing. Keep them weak and take advantage at every opportunity.

E13. Position on foreign relations with dictators
Dictators and monarchs are your natural allies. Appease them and call on them for assistance against your enemies. They will see it as a way to weaken your country's freedoms. You will then both have something on the other and be assured of secrecy.

E14. Position on protecting industry at the expense of the environment or public
Protecting the health of the public would have prevented the development of coal in West Virginia coal mines and hampered the expansion of a coast-to-coast rail system thru native and citizen-owned lands. Protecting poor Irish and Chinese building the railroad system is a bad idea. This is economic suicide. Industry must come first. Reduce expensive corporate regulation. They will reward you materially.

Protecting the health of the environment is a long-term gain but painful in the short term. Avoid it as you would for the protection of public health. Problems will eventually become obvious long after your reign & be someone else's problems. These are large complex problems whose blame can be spread around.

E15. Loyalists are arrested and imprisoned for wrongdoing

Referring to E5 above, you can reward loyalists with pardons. This will also prevent them from having to testify against you to reduce or eliminate their own sentences for crimes. Your enemies will criticize you; your supporters will see your loyalty; potential opponents will see the futility of opposing you and will go further in your service than their people will go in theirs.

Learning from your example, a conservative news commentator called on listeners to bail out the man who committed a home invasion of Speaker Pelosi's home and beat her husband in the head with a hammer. On this path, resist the decent impulse to apologize and instead *double down* on inciting violence against your opponents.

E16. Bureaucrats are more loyal to the country than to you personally

Classify these people as disloyal traitors. Even those who may have once done your service cannot be trusted if they place rules or the welfare of the country above your welfare. Destroy or replace them. This includes numerous judges, inspectors general, the FBI, and the Justice Department.

Count the number of Republican staff Trump fired in his brief four years for being more loyal to the country or the truth than him.

Trump attacked those actually knowledgeable

on any damaging issue.

Contradicted and ignore recommendations and warnings from Dr. Fauci on the covid-19 pandemic; dismissed masks, distancing, and told people to drink Clorox and inject Lysol. When people did and got sick or died, he said - on video - he bore no responsibility.

Withdrew the US from the World Health Organization - during the covid-19 pandemic.

Military leaders – attacked those criticizing his troop withdrawal from Syria, allowing Russia to crush the democratic reform movement there and gain him Russian support. Doubled-down by withdrawing troops from Germany to encourage the Russian invasion of democratic Ukraine.

Election Officials - call for their removal or arrest if they certify Biden.

Intelligence Services raising alarms about Libya & Russia must be slandered as working against America.

Attacked Governors and Mayors, allowing constitutionally protected peaceful protests against racial murder. Support those committing violence on your behalf, like Kyle Rittenhouse.

Attacks of peaceful protesters against racial murders with unmarked federal agents. Support the local police who shoot unarmed blacks and Hispanics who forget their second-class place.

In fact, he encouraged local police to shoot

additional black men on camera to turn peaceful protests violent, so he could then accuse them of being the real danger. Your followers want to believe that.

E17. You lose an election

If you see the writing on the wall ahead of the election, begin the emotional announcement that you know the opposition is going to commit fraud, even before the first vote is cast. Continue during and after the polling. When election irregularities are uncovered, it will sow doubt as to whom was responsible and to whether you really lost. This long list is well-documented and illustrative.

Afterward, state that the winner is not the winner, even if all legal challenges or lawsuits are lost. Therefore, you can declare yourself the winner by pressuring officials to 'recount' votes until you have won.

If even that fails, declare martial law and announce the election is invalid. Announce you will hold elections again as soon as the traitors are rooted out. Use this as the excuse to arrest and purge your opponents, some politically by not letting them take office, some by arrest and/ or assassination. Many rulers in the 20th and 21st centuries gained office in this manner.

In states confirming Biden won their electoral votes, Republican and Democrat officials side by side counted the votes. Many proceedings were videotaped. Ignore the facts like someone selling you swamp land in New Jersey.

Trump-appointed Attorney General Barr conceded that there was no evidence of widespread voter fraud. He was then attacked as disloyal. Remember, loyalty to you comes before the country.

Trump's call to suspend Constitution is not a 2024 deal-breaker, said House Republican Ohio Rep. Dave Joyce. He is right.

59 of 60 lawsuits accusing officials of fraud or error or otherwise discarding legitimate votes were dismissed. They lost the 60th after a full trial. Do you maintain the lie? Certainly. Who trusts the courts?

The FBI, responsible for internal US security at the federal level, stated there was no evidence of widespread voter fraud. They must be in league with secret democratic powers.

Republican election officials in disputed states, such as Georgia, all certified that the votes were accurate and without fraud. Go after them individually in the next election cycle. A lesson to the rest.

Trump continued to accuse Democrats of fixing the election results. No evidence exists, but none is required to make the accusation. Have others repeat the accusations often and loudly

4.

Notes on elections: what to do and what to look out for in your opposition

- Republican party in California installed its own ballot collection machines to throw away votes for the opposition.
- Texas limiting voting in democratic counties by removing all but one ballot deposit box.
- Reduced registration of voters in areas where you are not popular:

Online registration system 'crashed' amidst record numbers of registrations resulting in thousands of voters not registered in Florida, Georgia, and Oklahoma. Trump-appointed judges refused to extend the registration period to make up for downtime.

- Encourage uniformed police to go to voting sites wearing your campaign caps or buttons or shirts (illegal) to intimidate minorities. Encourage radical groups to do the same.

- Trump attorneys sue in court to have mail-in ballots counted by Nov 3 or discarded.
- Trump attorneys sue in court to have election results overturned.
- Trump attorneys sue to have his Vice President (Pence) ignore the electoral votes and declare him President.
- Trump demanded Governors or state legislatures dismiss the legitimate electors within a state and appoint people loyal to you.

- Trump, knowing democrats believe the truth of covid infection so are voting by mail in record numbers installed a political donor who never worked for the post office to be in charge & who owns businesses that compete with the post office.

Result: Saturday delivery eliminated, sorting machines taken offline, overtime canceled at peak voting period, fire middle management, and otherwise massively delayed mail so votes would not arrive in time. Very effective.

-tell lies which are immediately believed by core followers with no proof and which, therefore, cannot be refuted; based on fear and prejudice

-say those who have spoken against him have broken the law; presents no evidence

-say the other side has conducted massive voter fraud; presents no evidence

-accuse democrats of being pedophiles and sheltering them (best friend Epstein)

-attack your own people when they tell you no (Barr, firings, etc.)

-accuse peaceful racial equality protesters of being violent extremists

-tell violent police they are doing a great job of encouraging violence

-tell private militias and vigilantes they are fine people and patriots

-intimidate protesters by use of police & secret federal agents kidnapping protesters

-attempt intimidation of protesters by employing the national guard (under Trump, they balked)
-attempt intimidation of protesters by the military (under Trump, they balked)
-accuses the media of belonging to a secret underground deep state
-walk out of interviews when asked about your lies
-take no responsibility for people acting on what he says to do
-when asked about his lies at press conferences, accuses whoever is asking you of having an agenda & ban them from future conferences
-have leaders of media outlets subpoenaed to be grilled before the Republican senate
-perform running disinformation commentaries on social media;
complain of suppression by biased media when you are fact-checked and found lying.
-supports radical groups like Qanon, which without evidence, accuses and attacks your enemies
-pre-empts future investigations by placing doubt that the media is fair or competent
-pay a doctor to say he was unfit for military duty to avoid the draft
-pay to graduate college, where tests are taken and term papers are written by others.
-say those who have spoken against him have broken the law & should be arrested

-refuse to release tax records like every other President has done; court-ordered records confirmed Trump paid no taxes in 5 of 10 past years.

-call yourself a law and order man when encouraging police to perform violence against minorities;

They act on your behalf, knowing they have the support of either the Mayor,

Governor or the President and are unlikely to be prosecuted, even if caught on video.

5.

<u>Lies and other motivations for your base</u>

Lie about your political opposition planning violence

Lie about Biden raising taxes on average workers

Lie about violent blacks invading the suburbs

Lie about the police force being disbanded

Lie about whole cities like Portland are in flames already

Lie in March about covid being over in 15 days, over by Easter, over by summer

Lie that we have so many cases because we test more than anyone

- we don't & testing does not make people infected; it just finds them

Lies that he is a great businessman when his casinos, university, this & that all went

bankrupt draining his father's inheritance. Admired he was just a conman who ran circles

around businessmen and bankers in his first book.
Lies that he is a genius at negotiation when enemy nations play him for a fool (examples)
Trump punished states who did not vote for him by denying federal PPE gear and vaccine
Trump punished his political opponent by loaded incompetent friends to key positions instead of anyone qualified with experience
Trump punishing the country by ignoring covid and allowing 50 governors to pursue whatever approach they want disjointedly: covid preferentially will kill off the elderly & blacks
Trump called to Ukraine to bargain congressionally approved military aid for an investigation into the Bidens, a fact verified by the president's own acting chief of staff. Yet another reason to remove troops from Germany and encourage Putin.
Trump, in May, claimed that the US mortality rate, which at the time was 24.66 deaths per 100,000 people, and Germany's mortality rate, which then was 9.24 per 100,000, were the best in the world. In fact, a slew of other countries had lower mortality rates at the time.
Trump, in December, highlighted Germany's spike in COVID-19 deaths arguing that Germany's the pandemic response wasn't a model for the US, even though their death rate is 24.12/100,000 and the USA is 87.49: just because you

were caught lying, don't stop.

Note that being caught in all these illegal, immoral, and unethical activities and statements did NOTHING to alter the rabid support of his base. Both religious and secular leaders knew their views would never be condoned by any other national figure, so they instructed their followers to turn a blind eye to all their sins. Deny, deny, deny.

In the aftermath, instead of being ridden out of politics or simply tarred & feathered, Trump supporters seized Georgia voting data in a raid organized by Sidney Powell. Supporters stormed into a Georgia election office and absconded with voter data at the direction of Sidney Powell, according to a new report.

An examination by the Washington Post shows that Powell, a former Trump lawyer, helped organize the alleged breach in rural Coffee County and paid for the operation through her nonprofit, which at the time listed Michael Flynn among its directors, and the team she directed allegedly copied data from voting machines that have been misrepresented as "proof" of the former president's election fraud lies.

Courts or state lawmakers at least twice gave Trump supporters access to the machines, which are considered by the federal government to be "critical infrastructure," and local authorities in at least six other counties in four states gave non-authorized people access to voting machines or their data.

Remember, with every outrageous action or success, those on the fence or even opposed to you will fear you all the more. Power feeds on power. Do what the opposition shudders to even conceive.

Chapter 5

THE PERSONAL TOUCH

Even a leader dedicated to saying and doing whatever it takes to gain and maintain power can fail. There is one more skill set and by many accounts the most important.

Personal Aura
As CNN's Harwood put it: "Republicans in 2020 would 'go smack their moms in the face' if Trump ordered them to." In truth, this only applies to 25% - 40% of registered Republicans, but that's more than enough to control the party as long-term congressmen were afraid of that motivated core turning on them during primaries or not turning out to vote in the general election at a word from Trump.

A couple in Texas listened to Trump say they should swallow Clorox and inject Lysol to combat covid-19; he went to intensive care, and she died. Sadly, they were far from alone. When asked afterward about his responsibility to them, he relied, "I am not responsible. No."

The followers of Jim Jones willingly fed hundreds of their own children poisoned Koolaid before, as instructed, taking their own lives.

German citizens who for decades had gone to school and peacefully worked beside the Hebrews among them, knowing they were among the smartest in their community in banking and medicine, easily stood by idly and watched Hitler-inspired militia destroy Hebrew homes and places of worship, rape their women, burn down their businesses and round them up for slave labor and/or extermination. It is always dangerous to be a capable minority who can be blamed for the troubles of the many idiots.

This level of cultist obedience is not terribly difficult to employ, but much like the game of chess, few can master it. Those who do cannot be touched by mere dilatants politicians, who possess only one or two of the keys to such a level of obedience and belief.

Let us review the recorded discussion held by an Egyptian noble in the city of Pompeii when that doomed island community yet prospered. As you may know, the Egyptians had a developed, multicultural civilization and mathematics (they invented "0") before the Greeks. In turn, the Greeks developed philosophy into fine art and supplanted them, but both were ultimately overcome by the force of arms from Rome. The intellectuals in power never see the obvious coming to crush them.

The story is as old as politics itself. There are leaders like Alexander who march at the head of their armies into battle, inspiring the troops to greater valor and die young themselves. And there are the wiser leaders who privately mock but publicly applaud such service. Trump fired many of his staff when they heard him behind closed doors – this firing discredits anything they might know.

The techniques listed above under 'Principles' and 'Methodology' are enough to cow the herd, the cattle that make up the backbone of any movement. But what of the more intelligent among them? What of those who not only have technical ability but who have risen to be leaders in communities, churches, state government, and even national politics? Can they be swayed?

Of course, many can. Especially now, with modern psychoanalytic tools.

Take the example of Christopher Wylie - Cambridge Analytica whistleblower. The company, in a very technical and overt manner, sought to identify mental weaknesses in subject populations to better exploit said weaknesses to instill in them fake news and conspiracy theories and to motivate them to illegal actions. Even armed revolt against an existing government. Study these tools and employ professionals in this field to control men and women who are otherwise, by all outward appearances, intelligent, educated, and strong-willed individuals. This company, in particular, is a psychological operations web behemoth incarnated by Steve Bannon and backed by Robert and Rebekah Mercer. It is effective if you have the stomach for it. A fascist must in this media-laden century.

Wylie, who served as Cambridge Analytica's research director for a year and a half, watched as his group began to use data from Facebook and other online sources to target users for disinformation campaigns. "They targeted people who were more prone to conspiratorial thinking," Wylie says. "They used that data, and they used social media more broadly, to first identify those people, and then engage those people, and really begin to craft what, in my view, was an insurgency in the United States." Wylie adds: "The things that I was building on originally for the defense of our democracies had been completely inverted to really, in my view, attack our democracies." Wylie's new book, Mindf*ck, explains how Cambridge Analytica harvested the information of tens of millions of Facebook users, then used the data to target people susceptible to disinformation, racist thinking, and conspiracy theories.

Though Cambridge Analytica no longer (publically) exists, Wylie warns that the company's tactics continue to be a threat to democracy. He notes that some of its former employees are currently working on the next Trump campaign. Money and status will bring many professionals into your fold who do not share the values of any particular movement. They just want money or power or both. Imagine such an effort today augmented by fake A.I. voice and video clips!

Beginning with Cambridge University research, it later became Cambridge Analytica. Essentially it began identifying people in the same way that you'd be looking for people who'd be more vulnerable to ISIS messaging — people who were more prone to conspiratorial thinking or paranoid ideation. Effectively, it looks for the same kinds of people. But rather than discouraging them from joining ISIS, it would be to encourage them to join the alt-right.

Some professionals, like R. Guliani of New York, were once respected and in the national limelight for a short time. They were stars and loved the attention. And grew despondent when their subsequent life did not present them with that emotional high. These are easy to convince with the arguments, since while intellectually it may be recognized as manipulation, their emotional self recognizes an opportunity to once again shine on a national or even international stage.

Some in politics are intelligent but either naive or inexperienced, or both. If you lie long enough, sincerely passionate enough, and claim to understand a world they find complex, confusing, hypocritical, or unfair, you will seem a great man to them. *A genius of the human condition.* And with enough apparent successes behind you, which you make sure everyone knows of, even if you have to stretch the truth of your resume, you can even go around calling yourself a genius. Do so, especially in venues where there is no one to actively contradict you. This may require stacking the audience behind you with known or paid supporters.

What you said and the cheers of the crowd will be reported. No matter what caveats are added or fact-checking is employed, the *emotional impact* on the lost, the weak, the naive, and the uneducated will be *far more meaningful.* Keep this in mind when you pack your rallies and public audiences with followers & believers. Addressing a genuine neutral sample of the public can be dangerous, leading to a hasty exit on your part before too much is said or people have a chance to hear more from those concerned with your policies. Trump followed Hitler in making this error several times as they improved.

This brings to mind the subject of debates: a bad idea. If the culture in which you find yourself embraces this archaic ritual, you, unfortunately, must appear to warmly embrace it. Once there, however, use it as a platform to unreservedly attack your opponent verbally. Interrupt them at every opportunity, and ignore the rules of the debate. It helps if, going into the debate, your opponent looks upon you as a rabid dog who may explode if confronted too directly. Something new rarely comes out of modern American debates, but fireworks are always appreciated by *your ignorant supporters*. You will lose nothing in their eyes and possibly sow doubt into those who were *mildly supporting your passionless opponent*, that he is weak, uninformed, or a fool who cannot stand up for himself.

A group of politicians attaching themselves to you who actually think and control large blocks of others are true Machiavellians. They will not believe your nonsense for one moment but will publicly and loudly support you once they see how the common man responds to you. Such are 47 of 50 Republican senators. Such was DeJoy, who donated over a million dollars to Trump and was rewarded by allowing him to dismantle US Post Office operations, which profited from his own competing postal business interests. Trump was an atheist who caused plenty of abortions among young, vulnerable women, but that didn't stop him from championing a rabid evangelist like M. Pence as his vice president. As an added bonus, having someone like him as your number two may be enough to hold off those who would remove you by assassination or impeachment, fearing what would follow from your martyrdom.

Assassination as policy at lower and midlevel elections is more common than realized outside Hollywood movies. Just saying.

The more of the apparent 'intelligencia' you can sway to your cause, the more of a genius you shall seem. Perhaps like Christian leaders, they have one goal only - in their case, eliminating the scourge of abortion by sympathetic judicial appointments. Perhaps like Gulliani, their star doesn't quite shine like it once did, or they themselves failed to attain the heights to which your movement now seems destined. Or perhaps they are pragmatists like Ted Cruz or shiftless Senators like Graham who realize you have the rabid core voting block in your back pocket and can (and do) turn them viciously on anyone opposing you. Ruthlessness is your friend, especially when used against one-time supporters.

This leads to preparation in setting up another mindset among the intellectuals while feeding the bloodlust of the proletariat: fire people. Do it early. Do it often. Do it to high-profile people or people who are renowned experts in their area. Trust me, and it will not backfire on you. In fact, it raises your stature to fire or insult those who have, through hard-earned training, intellect, and years of ethical service to something other than themselves, have a certain standing. Trust that this kind of standing is always on thin ice, ready to be burst by *something the common man can understand* and to which they can relate. And feel better about themselves. And confirm their fears.

Those who dwell on talking numbers and percentages are doomed to watch their audience's eyes cross and glaze. Even if one of them is not your enemy, and may even have supported you, jump on the opportunity to humiliate them, and the common man will love you for it.

Remember, you will never have the support of a free press, so suppress or distract it at any opportunity. You will never have the support of the intellectual and well-educated community at large, so paint them as villains, anarchists, communists, pedophiles, godless souls who seek to profit by turning the {name a group they already hate or fear} loose to ravage your neighborhoods, your schools, your wives and daughters.

Just try not to laugh at followers when they cheer you for saying the most ridiculous things. Have you ever sat down and heard what they tell each other all day long? In the words of Cordero, the bandit, "If god had not intended them to be sheared, he would not have made them sheep!"

Public Speaking Techniques

It bears repeating that you are speaking to several distinct groups. Supporters and the weak-minded who look to you for strong, consistent leadership, the opposition who you will never convince of your correctness and righteousness, and others who are either too busy with their own lives to pay strong attention or simply are unsure of who is telling them the truth. Speak to the first group with energy, emotion and conviction and *you will sway or at least place doubt in the last group.* The middle group cannot be reached and should be ignored.

A recent historical example of developing an effective fascist speaker is seen in the rise of Adolph Hitler, a failed Austrian painter, into the most powerful public speaker of his time. Embracing the opportunity the nationalist socialist party of post-WWI Germany presented him, he began in coffee houses and other tiny public venues where he was often mocked, if not beaten, by the audience. Persistent, he improved his techniques and became more than just the spokesman for the growing, violent movement. He became its leader, publicly embracing all the attributes expected in such a leader. He like Trump grew in power too much for the old party heads to control. No surprise.

For the American example, we need to look no further than religious evangelists. Their techniques have been refined to pertain to a specific bible and reference to what they tell you the creator of the universe demands of you. They do so by interpreting the written word of the bible for you. Most people are religious or superstitious (rabbit feet, astrology, gods & an afterlife in one way or another) and fail at performing academic analysis themselves. They need priests. However, those who excel at academic analysis are generally mistrusted by the masses. When a speaker comes along who speaks their language, who tells them in 'plain language' who is to blame for misfortune in their lives, and who reflects their fears of strangers and those who look or believe differently than them, they can sell anything. Even telling you to inject Clorox. Huh? Even saying a South American dictator who died nine years earlier is responsible for helping rig the 2020 presidential election? What? Even saying the Democrats so cleverly rigged the election for Trump to lose but did not do so to make Republican congressmen lose as well? You're kidding! No, unfortunately we are not kidding. They believe and act, either by voting, protesting, or violence against those they identify as their enemies. And will love you for telling them the 'unvarnished truth.' For too many years politicians never answer a question clearly or directly. Their mealy-mouthed pandering on camera is obvious, seldom committing to an action, and for such losers a large segment of voters are never motivated to get off their couches. Give them passions, even unsupported ones.

A hereditary monarchy says a King is the best ruler since he is the son of kings. An aristocracy says the wealthy & children of those already in power know better than the common man. Democracy says common men can understand national and international complexities so they should have a say. Only fascism strips away the veneer used by other systems of governance and exposes what underlies all successful governments: strong-willed men and women who ignore, deceive and suppress the weak and stupid masses to achieve their ends. If those ends match the good of a nation, swell. If not, it still inspires an efficient form of governance. Look no further than Hitler raising a nation on its knees after a disastrous war to within a hairs breath of world domination and nuclear power.

A good speaker, one who is emotional and speaks to (a) people's fears and (b) selfishness will inspire followers far more than those who speak of brotherhood and kindness, charity and fairness. Children embraced the old Superman television series motto of "truth, justice, and the American way"; as adults those same children know better. And after generations of listening to multiple established party politicians ducking questions and speaking vaguely so that they can later say, "No, that's not what I meant," the refreshing directness of *a true fascist is emotionally attractive*. It does not matter if you are fact-checked on every speech as incorrect, a hate monger, or an outright liar. What matters is that they can relate to you, both the ignorant and the educated. Not everyone will relate to you, but you can ignore those citizens who do not since *they will never support you anyway*.

Remembering the words of the brilliant orator and writer Orson Wells, when confronted with the right or wrong of self interest over personal sacrifice, he reminded his listener of the greater good his selfish actions can cause.

"In Italy for 30 years under the Borgia they had warfare, murder, terror and bloodshed. They also had Michelangelo, Leonardo Davinci and the Renessaince. Meanwhile in Switzerland they had brotherly love. After 500 years of democracy and peace, what was the result? The cookoo clock!"

Special Local Conditions

Those who wish to lead the cattle in India have different ground rules than those so laboring in Iran, Israel, or elsewhere. Local conditions dictate the expressed 'beliefs' and alliances of the effective politician, fascist or not.

In 21st-century America, the overriding ground condition, the terrain upon which you operate is Christianity. In all its forms, in all disparity and hypocrisy, this is the underlying set of beliefs by which the cattle will judge you. It is openly believed, even by self-identified non-believers, that the USA was founded as a Christian nation, largely by Christians, such that even our money has the imprint of the god of Abraham being the expression of trust.

Here are the facts:

At its founding, Christian denominations dominated the 13 colonies.

At its founding, Native American religious practices were condemned as satanic.

Today, 74.3% believe in a deity (as do some of the 23% not denomination affiliated)

Today, 70.6% define themselves as Christians.

Today, 1.9% define themselves as Jews (the perfect high-achieving, low-population enemy)

Among Christians, evangelicals are the most aggressive.

Pole results indicate the vast majority of white evangelicals consider stance towards religious beliefs an important trait of a U.S. president, but only a third of them considered Trump to be religious. While Mike Pence was considered religious by 87% of white evangelicals, this was only 37% for Trump, and even Joseph Biden was considered a bit more religious.

There is great confusion as to why a Trump has such strong evangelical support. Simply put, it is because Trump's invocation of the decline of white Christian

America proved effective in activating religious identity threats in a way that led white evangelicals to coalesce around his candidacy. In this way, Trump's ability to articulate white evangelicals' fears about the declining influence of Christianity likely overrode any lingering concerns about his religiosity. His appointed judges were a promise kept.

Use this. You are not in Tehran, Tel Aviv, or Calcutta. Understand what motivates –really *motivates* – a Christian majority so clueless they believe we lost paradise because a rib woman listened to a talking snake and ate a magic apple, and you will prevail. *They themselves* will invent the rationales for your actions or lack of actions on any issue. Those rationales are NOT FOR YOU to preach. You shall preach to their *actual motivations* and, by doing so, confound your enemies.

Let us examine how the hypocritical leaders of evangelists rationalize and support you.

A group of far-right Christian nationalists known as the Black Robe Regiment is devoted to Donald Trump and, as expected, casted doubt on the 2022 election results. They are a modern-day group inspired by a myth of a group of militant pastors during the American Revolution who took up arms to lead their flock into battle against the British. The movement, imbued with support from far-right political activists like Michael Flynn, wants pastors to play a central role in not only preaching politics from the pulpit but also actively getting their congregations to rise and claim election fraud by weaving myths about the American Revolution. These pastors state they're saving democracy, though what they're doing is encouraging supporters to undermine the democratic process. His sermon mixed Bible verses with remarks about evolution, made claims of violence against anti-abortion groups, and described Jews as a 'wealthy group of people who don't believe in heaven or hell, didn't believe in angels, and they have political control over everything. Take lessons.

As with mainstream Republican politicians fearful of Trump, the vast majority of Christian pastors, ministers & priests are not rising against this blatant anti-christian movement. Anyone read the ten commandments lately? Violence, intimidation, lies, and deception worthy of Lucifer himself should have them all condemning the movement, but this tiny group – until recently less than the 2% of Americans who are Jews – *remains untouchable* by the hypocrites who look the other way, so their flocks will not abandon them. Just like politicians who do not believe for one minute the 2020 election was stolen but campaigned on it.

Trump has counted on this. In announcing his 2024 run, he stated, "Hopefully today will turn out to be one of the most important days in the history of our Country!" on Truth Social just hours after reposting an image shared by a platform user called "God_Bless_Trump" who posted a warning of demon gods taking charge of America.

That is what they needed to hear. The exceptions who speak up are best ignored by you as it reduces their publicity. Church Militant founder Michael Voris warned that, in the "all-out war going on between the forces of darkness who have complete control of one political party and partial control over the other," conservatives might have "no choice but to fight back violently if needs be." Get the rabid dogs on your side, and the sheep can be herded.

Welcome to a fallen world. This may be your best chance for power since Joe McCarthy in the 1950s.

Uses of Power

In America, as in other nations, certain agencies are tasked with the protection of the public and of the government itself. Regulators. Auditors. Prosecutors who watch those already in the seat of power. So how can you circumvent them for your gain?

President Trump had a brief four years but accomplished much. By Republicans stonewalling Supreme Court nominees in the years before he took office, his party ensured him the opportunity to control the majority of the aging court with his appointees. Less known was his clever appointment of allies and employees as federal judges at lesser levels throughout the federal government. From these appointees, court cases for his donors and supporters were and still are being swayed in their favor.

These kinds of favors are paid for and vital to a ruler. Another weapon of the Presidency seldom used to is fire or appoint special counsel watchdogs. Those who watch every level of the federal government, especially the executive branch, *were fired in record numbers.* Not just one or two here and there who came up against him, but a systematic pre-emptive attack. Cleverly, if a suitable supporter could not be placed in the position, it was left vacant. For years. This completely circumvents the due process of review, which kept many of his more obvious political friends and servants from such positions.

Effectively, it achieved the same ends.

Trickle-down deregulation of industries in which you or your supporters operate as civilian businessmen is illustrative. Three judges appointed by former President Donald Trump handed down an astonishing decision in October 2022, long after he was out of office, effectively holding that the Consumer Financial Protection Bureau, the federal agency charged with protecting consumers from a wide range of predatory activity by lenders and other financial services, is unconstitutional and must be stripped of its authority. By doing so, it crippled the protection of consumers by unscrupulous businessmen, even those not personally involved with Trump. Thus it has far-reaching harm to the country and its citizens. But who cares? As long as *your business needs* are cared for, there will always be necessary collateral damage. In politics, as in war, this is just a price for victory which the strong must pay. Your important business and corporate supporters will thank you. And opponents will be vigorously punished by your supporters for doing so. For example, Karpov was a "Putin ultra-loyalist" before criticizing the Russian leader over his invasion of Ukraine. At one point during the invasion, Karpov reportedly called upon Putin to end the war against Ukraine "so that peaceful people will stop dying." 71-year-old Anatoly Karpov was hospitalized on Oct 30, 2022 after allegedly "suffering a fall." He then resided in the neurology ward with mysterious multiple head and neck injuries in a coma. A splendid example of how an assassination is not the only weapon of choice for rabid supporters. Claims by witnesses he was attacked outside their parliament building are derided as "fake news." Such efforts intimidate critics and encourage your more violent followers without a simple death. Karpov was just the latest of over 40 former Putin allies to end up dead or seriously injured following Putin's second invasion of Ukraine in February 2022.

Chapter 6

SELECT QUOTATIONS FROM 2022

Be a leader of the times in which you live. You must speak to those who already support you and others who will respect your strength & conviction, saying what they believe but have been discouraged from saying out loud in the liberal, cattle-controlled times from President Johnson's great society of the 1960s until 2000.

Winner Quotations
Donald Trump - During an appearance on CNN's "State of the Union," his threatening social media post claimed Senate Minority Leader Mitch McConnell

(R-KY) has, as Trump put it, a "DEATH WISH." Trump followed up with a racial slur about his wife.

It's just what his violent base loved. Not a single Republican senator came out against it.

They were afraid to be abandoned in their next primary or election.

Donald Trump stated, "No President has done more for Israel than I have. Somewhat surprisingly, however, our wonderful Evangelicals are far more appreciative of this than the people of the Jewish faith, especially those living in the U.S. ... Jews have to get their act together and appreciate what they have in Israel - *Before it is too late!*"

Spot on the money. If your hardcore base is his white, redneck evangelicals, their known dislike of Jews to begin with, this tells them they are right. That liberal, left-wing Jews are ungrateful. And deserving of the general derision against them. And soon they'll be dealt with!

Lauren Boebert - "Colorado deserves a fighter who will stand up for freedom, who believes in America, and who is willing to take on all the left-wing lunatics who are trying so hard to ruin our country. We are in a battle for the heart and soul of our country."

Very effective.

Lauren Boebert is an unapologetic "Christian nationalist" who believes America should be guided by a specific set of religious beliefs. At one event, Boebert came right out and said, "I'm tired of this separation of church and state junk that's *not in the Constitution.*"

She spoke from the heart what many feel.

"God told me it would be a sign and a wonder to the unbeliever" to defeat a five-term incumbent, Boebert said — suggesting that her unlikely win might turn non-Christians to her religion. Truly inspiring, getting many who never have trouble to vote off their couches. Bravo.

Rep. Mike Johnson presented Republicans with a way to deny the 2020 election result without having to lean into more extreme claims of voter fraud:

He touted "credible allegations of fraud" and "rigged" voting machines.

Johnson gave the GOP a defense for rejecting the 2020 election that doesn't rely on extreme allegations. Without advanced college degrees, just what do you think the common man thought when he said those things? Yeah, spot on!

"No one's ever fucked with a candidate as we've fucked with a candidate," Lincoln Project co-founder Rick Wilson says early in the doc; those schemes include a Times Square billboard, attention-getting for attention's sake. "You are reaching an emotional resonance with people," Wilson tells an exhausted video editor who doesn't want to use footage of George Floyd's grieving family in an advert. "It's not exploitative."

Brilliant. It's been said that former President Donald Trump corrupts all who enter his orbit — that it's impossible to deal directly with him without taking on his amorality and crassness.

"The Lincoln Project," a documentary series on Showtime, depicts that process among his political opposition. Here, people devoted to ousting Trump mirror his rhetorical style and his self-regard. And it's subtly making this case that the documentary succeeds, even as it grows punishing to watch.

Rand Paul says outright on video that political opponent Booker "doesn't believe in civil discourse, only violence." He accuses the Black former state lawmaker of associating with members of the "radical left" who condone and perpetuate violence. He does not make the mistake of faking evidence (there is none) and just states the lie convincingly, knowing it is false.

The video released is an excellent preemptive attack against Booker shortly before the Democratic challenger to his senate seat appeared at a campaign forum aired on statewide television. Take lessons.

Florida Governor Ron DeSantis stated, "They Should Not Be Here At All," claiming the majority of post-hurricane looters are illegal immigrants. He selected a particular group of 4 people arrested where 3 of them were illegal, ignoring the majority of looters were American citizens. He surrounded himself with police and other fascists in uniform during the press conference video.

A wonderful example of making hay on a completely unrelated topic – immigration – to

1. divert attention from his trying to defund FEMA then asking it for money when a hurricane hit in late 2022

2. support his transporting immigrants from Texas to New England.
3. reinforce his support by police departments.

Tucker Carlson, a media influencer, stated Victory for the Democrats, and hence for a multiracial democracy, would be "atrocity and barbarism," "subjugation or extermination," or "white genocide."

> What the Confederates did after losing the civil war, the Republicans are doing now. For the Confederates, white freedom was Black enslavement. Black freedom was white enslavement. For modern Republicans, the pattern is the same.
>
> A lovely and historic renewal of binary thinking. Anything good for blacks must be bad for whites, contrary to the idea of multi-racial democracy strengthening us all.

Lara Logan was an award-winning newscaster giving an unhinged rant on Newsmax: a Satanic "global cabal" that must be defeated by White Christians, regurgitating Q-Anon talking points including the racist "Great Replacement" conspiracy theory, insisting she had proof of a worldwide plan to fully implement in the United States. That escalated to talk of Satan and non-Republicans who "dine on the blood of children."

> Finding allies among unhinged extremists is essential. You may know better, but for every extremist with genuine god fantasies, there is a

hard core of folks who think the same things. Flat Earth. Moon landings a hoax. Earth is 6,000 years old. Those folks are never motivated by mealy-mouthed centrist politicians. You need these rabid dogs to bring out the vote. You can deny without denying. Just keep giving them platforms on which to speak, let them join your rallies, and the unwashed idiots with get the message: you approve. Trust me. They will *never* vote for the other side.

In this case, the other side for Republicans are baby-eating, demon-worshiping leftist-progressive liberals. And every time you label an opponent 'leftist-progressive liberals,' they will hear 'baby eating, demon worshipers.'

Well done, Lara.

Loser Quotations
"Newsmax condemns in the strongest terms the reprehensible statements made by Lara Logan," the network said in a statement shared with The Daily Beast on Thursday. "We have no plans to interview her again."

> The mostly far-right news network has banned her from its airwaves despite Eric Bolling having brought her on his show, saying, "a good friend of the show and a good friend of mine as well."
>
> He gave her the platform to speak in "free-

speech" America, then punished her for using it when his job & money was at stake. Beware: let this be a lesson to you if you ever feel you have gone too far in abusing 'free speech' with your lies. There is *no such thing* as free speech. Everything has a price in a democracy. Money and power win, not intellectual ideas of justice & loyalty.

Liz Cheney said that Arizona GOP candidates threaten democracy. "In Arizona recently, you had a candidate for governor in Kari Lake, you have a candidate for Secretary of State in Mark Finchem, both of whom have said — this isn't a surprise, it's not a secret — they both said that they will only honor the results of an election if they agree with it," Cheney told her audience.

>The desire to win is paramount. How can someone be criticized for never giving up? Truly the quintessential American spirit, which Cheney lacks. Their actions match well with their inspiration, Trump, who learned how effective this can be in the business world, habitually refusing to make contracted payments and only honoring costly agreements after being sued: it saved him millions when the opposition settled for less or outright lost in court! While Trump is a spoiled, childish bully who occasionally loses control, he's not wrong in embracing the lessons of his KKK father, Fred Trump. Attorneys are your troops in that war.

The same pertains to politics. A rotation in politicians in America happens periodically without violence or force, but regime change – real change – requires these things. Motivating political followers to violent overthrow is no more difficult than getting Christians to ignore the 'ten commandments,' killing millions in the Crusades, or burning young women to death as witches. The denial and blame others for what you are doing techniques are used to turn the cattle into wolves.

Cheney further said she saw firsthand, working overseas, how fragile foreign democracies are. "And I think I knew on some level that even in the United States this was fragile," she said. "But I certainly didn't understand just how fragile. I think that's such an important lesson that we need to take from history."

That's honest of her. She did not understand that giving everyone a voice despite race, color, or creed is not the natural state of man, and he will eventually throw off those unnatural shackles in favor of the rule of the strong over the weak, victory by intimidation or violence, and sincere self-interest.

Conservative pundit Scott Jennings said Trump had sent "assassination instructions" about McConnell.

Jennings said, "Every Republican ought to be able to say" that Trump's post was "beyond the pale."

"This is bad for the party," Jennings said.

Typical of losers, this one-time Republican

rails about injustice and failures to adhere to the old law during a regime change. No regime change happens without this – the law is defined by the winners. Caesar's lament after he slaughtered opponents in the Punic wars was not 'I came, I saw, I conquered,...I feel really bad about it.' *No, he did not.* Revel in your enemy's demolition.

Democratic opponent to Senator Rand Paul, a black man named Booker, accused Paul of "blowing the dog whistle" on public safety and policing issues. Paul's campaign and his allies had tried to connect Booker with the "defund the police" movement. "Rand Paul wants people to look at the color of my skin instead of my record," Booker said.

While absolutely true, his defense against baseless accusations cannot be proved any more than the false accusations of violence against him. Remember this technique as one of the best ways to attack your opponents: accuse them of something – without a shred of proof – and laugh as they scramble to 'clear the air.' The technique is broadly *"No one can disprove a negative."*

Example: "When there's a crisis, when someone's in an emergency, we all want to call 911 and have someone in law enforcement come to our aid," Booker said. "What we don't need is that same agency we call to protect and serve us, kick in our door, and shoot us in the dead of night."

Immediately after, Paul accused Booker of trying to *defund the police*! Brilliant.

Hershel Walker, ex-football star and political candidate, claimed he was pro-life and anti-abortion. This fit with the Republican and Christian demographic he was courting. When asked why he was departing the campaign for a while: "People don't know that I have this food service company; I have a drapery company, and I supervise six hospitals around the United States," he said.

None of it true.

Records show he paid for his girlfriend's abortion in an out-of-wedlock pregnancy.

Medical records show he dropped another lover at her abortion clinic.

Records show he does not and has never supervised six hospitals & flashed a fake police badge during a debate.

Afterward, he was neck and neck in his race for Congress & continues to have party support.

Let this be a lesson for those who seek power: claiming that Jewish space lasers caused the California fires to make bankers rich is ok to say. It inspires fear on the chance it's true and cannot be proved either way. Again, *"No one can disprove a negative"*. And encourages other extremists to float their own wacky ideas. Empowering.

However, Walker's idiotic claim embellishing his resume could easily be checked, as was the bill he paid for the abortion. Your constituents sometimes care about such things, so be smart.

He ended up hurting his party only a small amount. After the above Walker revelations came out in 2022, the party continued to support him and are quoted on video saying, "Character doesn't matter." Then "National security doesn't matter." And finally, "Abortion doesn't matter. *Nothing but power matters.*" Walker is a black Republican, so they support him to confuse the enemy (black voters). Black Republican leaders know better, but just like Adam Clayton Powell in the 1960s, they keep their fellow black Americans distracted for their own power.

While absolutely true, you cannot say so to the cattle. Eventually, some of them will wake up, feel betrayed, and turn on you with their votes. Many Christian evangelists stayed with Trump, not because they believed the lip service he gave to their beliefs, but because he put their anti-abortion, book-burning judge candidates on the bench at all levels of government. It's all about power, yes, but you must maintain the image. The illusion. Else you open the door to another candidate in your party who can call you out on it like DeSantis breaking with Trump in 2022. So be smart. Be consistent.

Miller (former Republican strategist) was asked who among current Republicans in late 2022 best embodies the party's 'abject nihilism or cynicism.' He didn't hesitate to name Rep. Elise Stefanik (R-NY), a formerly moderate Republican who became an ultra-MAGA hardliner after former President Donald Trump's election.

"To me, she is the worst because it's just the most brazen," he said. "It also is the worst at some level because *it's paying off for her*. I truly think she'll be on a VP shortlist for Trump 'cause he'll want a woman if he runs in 2024. And if not that, I think she's on a speaker of the house trajectory."

> This loser Miller did not recognize Stefanik for who she was when she claimed to be a moderate Republican before 2018. She even fooled professionals like him, as that role was the one that brought her to power. Even now, he fails to understand winning when the climate goes rabid. She does not.

Conservative rabbi Shmuley Boteac has some harsh words for Republicans and their silence on Rep. Marjorie Taylor Greene (R-GA) and what he describes as her "Jew hatred."

Earlier this year, Greene attended the America First Political Action Conference organized by a man the ADL called a 'prominent white supremacist pundit' and is a Holocaust denier who said, "Jews burning in gas chambers was like baking cookies," he writes. "After being criticized for speaking at the conference where Vladimir Putin and Adolf Hitler were praised, Greene doubled down and blamed the bad publicity she got on Democrats and 'Pharisees in the Republican Party.' McCarthy again was silent."

Clearly, this Republican rabbi had no idea of reality in 2022. She further states, "Republicans may think it is good politics to change the subject by talking about the Democrats, but they only succeed in looking like hypocrites. Although it is late, it is not too late for the GOP to condemn Greene outright before the plague of anti-semitism spreads. Marjorie Taylor Greene must be ostracized by the Republican Party."

This thinking reflects the republican party under Ronald Regan in the 1980s, not the party of today. This hypocrisy is exactly what is giving renewed energy to Republicans, as fascism is now openly encouraged while giving lip services to equality and fairness. The rabbi is out of touch, hence her surprise and astonishment at the Republican leadership's inaction. Greene brings out the extremists not only in her voting district but nationwide. They now have a voice, and it is not that of the inept Democrats or old-school Republicans.

Texas Secretary of State John Scott (R) decried the "absurd" amount of threats faced by election workers in recent years, pointing the finger at conspiracy theorists such as Alex Jones. "That behavior is unacceptable under any scenario," Scott said of the threats.

> "Just because somebody said something or they saw something on TV, that doesn't excuse it."

Not only is such behavior acceptable, but it is also required when your political party is outnumbered nationwide. As former President Trump said on camera, "If everyone were allowed to vote, no Republican would ever be elected again." The tactics of intimidation, threats, and occasional violence to make the threats credible are core to winning. Do you want to win or not, Mr. Scott?

He shows a spectacular lack of vision.

Maj. Gen. Patrick Donahoe responded after Fox News host Tucker Carlson took to the airwaves to ridicule female service members. He defended the tens of thousands of women in the ranks in a social media post.

> The general has had his retirement delayed and now reportedly faces the possibility of censure and other punishment. The army rebuked Donahoe for statements on behalf of female soldiers — as well as others defending long-standing military vaccination policies — that have brought "negative publicity" to the military. It also assesses that he "failed to display Army values and core leader competencies."
>
> The Army is essentially broadcasting that it may kowtow to disingenuous partisan attacks rather than defend its troops and their leaders. Fox News' Laura Ingram, called him a "woke",

a "leftist troll." A conservative website also charged that his Twitter response to the threatened female soldier, his subordinate, amounted to "grooming his slut."

During the current rise of evangelical fascism in America, just as happened in Italy and Nazi Germany, the wise will keep their mouths shut and allow anything in the name of patriotism.

Jewish writer Tal Levin published an article condemning Kayne West inciting hatred against Jews, entitled "Kanye West's anti-semitic rants are the tip of a much longer spear." It was lucid, intelligent, and well thought out. It cited numerous references and quotes which could be checked with minimal effort. Very accurate.

Wasted effort. The comments of readers online ranged from blindly refusing to believe West said these things, or saying it's just words so Jews should grow a thicker skin after 2000 years, or admiration for how Kanye is brave enough to speak the truth. The kind of people who love to hate & blame someone else for their troubles – and that's half of humanity – will never let the facts get in the way of their hatred. Use this.

Words of losers like Levin are spit on a forest fire and have been forever. As only 2% of the population, Jews are despised for being smart and well-educated. All the Jewish doctors healing people and lawyers guarding civil rights make no dent in hatred. All the haters can see are people *different than them living better than they are.*

The final example of loser thinking comes just before this manual was published. Rep. Marjorie Greene characterized Pelosi's husband being violently attacked in her home by an assailant looking for her as an example of President Biden's failed America putting Greene in danger. Democratic Rep. Jim McGovern denounced Rep. Greene and blamed her for calling for Pelosi's execution in the past. "YOU called for Nancy Pelosi to be executed. YOU said she should be hung for treason," the Massachusetts lawmaker tweeted. "And now that someone listened, you're making Paul Pelosi's attack about YOU. This is what Republicans stand for, America. It's sick."

> It is opportunism and clear thinking. She inspires. Greene is adhering to her agenda of blaming the opposition when she attacks them and encourages violence against them. Is this not how revolutions are conducted? Is there a single nation on Earth that sprung into existence without violence? Someone has to lose: make sure it's not you. McGovern is not up to the task of defending the status quo of liberalism. Prominent conservatives like Charlie Kirk have got what it takes. He called on his audience to bail out Pelosi's attacker.

Chapter 7

CONCLUSIONS & EXECUTIVE SUMMARY

Using the military to police Americans flies in the face of U.S. traditions and values — and violates a long-standing principle known as 'posse comitatus.' More than a century ago, Congress passed the Posse Comitatus Act to ban the use of federal troops for law enforcement purposes not expressly authorized by law.

But Trump and Attorney General William Barr have found a way around the act. Federal agents and the military were used to kidnap, beat, and arrest protesters in DC and Portland was just, Trump and Barr proclaimed, "training." Congress was advised to act quickly to close this loophole before more communities start looking like war zones.

The loophole still exists, waiting for Trump or someone else with the strength to take the Presidency. Along the way, the ground must be prepared for winning hearts and minds. We recommend the following precepts.

C1. A lie that serves you is better than a truth that does not.

C2. It is better to be feared than anything else.

C3. The path to winning is by total domination.

C4. A nation where every citizen believes he is empowered to be a soldier and patriot is undefeatable. You pull their strings & sanction their atrocities.

C5. Liberalism is a weakness. It drains power directly from the powerful for the indirect benefit of the weak. They don't appreciate it anyway.

C6. That which is not actively helping you is actively opposing you.

C7. If everyone were allowed to vote, the strong would never hold power.

C8. Everyone can be driven to fear that which is different. Divide them and conquer.

C9. Take no responsibility for your failures.
Take all credit for that which succeeds.

C10. Turn every event into an opportunity to reinforce your position.

C11. Understand the frightened, weak cattle you are dealing with:

20% of the population cannot locate America on a map

20% of the population cannot name who we declared independence from

20% of the population believe witches in league with satan are real

20% of the population believe the sun revolves around Earth: God made it that way

20% of the population believe the lottery is a sound financial investment

20% of the population believes in alien abductions

25% of Americans believe God influences the outcome of the Superbowl & pray for it.

12 million Americans believe lizard people run the country.

As many Americans believe in Big Foot as in the Big Bang.

50% of Americans believe global warming will harm America, but not them personally.

Understand the math: separate groups of 20% believe in the above, with some modest overlap. So we are not talking about 20% x 300 million = 60 million people, but 2 or 3 times that number added together. Certainly half the voting population. These people will believe whatever truth you make appealing to them.
- they are superior
- they are righteous and chosen by God
- they are unfairly attacked by everyone else

- they are moral and ethical
- they deserve a better life
- *someone is to blame for denying them a better life (key)*

C12. Chose your verbal idiocy and stick to it:
- Many voters believe a race of giants once roamed the Earth, the result of women and angels interbreeding.
- Many voters believe evil spirits can control people
- Many voters believe there will be an afterlife in which exactly 144,000 people get to live eternally in Paradise
- Many voters believe the process that produced this world and human life is best unveiled not by the scientific method but by the musings of iron age herdsmen or con artists whose theories are best judged by examining *assertions that cannot be falsified.* (brilliant)
- Many voters think chocolate milk comes from brown cows
- Many voters believe dinosaurs and people existed at the same time

Think about who you are dealing with. The reason a Hershel Walker, Tucker Carlson, Marjorie Greene, or Donald Trump continue to gather voters and fans in large numbers are the very statements that their opponents scoff at and too easily dismiss. By making these wild claims (Jewish space lasers, chips to control you inserted into vaccines, America blew up the

European pipeline, etc.), they allow those with even wilder beliefs than the millions noted above to come out of hiding. Those people will be encouraged to join in a political movement – especially a violent one – in which they never previously believed they had a stake or could have a voice. They may never believe in Judaic space lasers causing forest fires in California, but as long as you never waiver in your outrageous statements, they will respect and support your idiocy. Because they feel you support *their* idiocy. Their entitlement.

Their lot in life is your opponents' fault, not their own.

Once you have the support of such people, they will absolutely defend, if not believe everything else you say on the murky political or social front:

- the election was stolen from us
- those in power now lie about us – are pedophiles – out to harm us – want to control us
- you know the best way to hold elections, not those now in power
- you know the best way to educate the young & what books and ideas are harmful
- you know which lifestyles are morally corrupt and will destroy the country
- you know which overseas countries – especially repressive dictatorships – have the right idea

C13. Most importantly, embrace the truth of voters
Time and again, the successful fascist will hear his

supporters loudly condemn the opposition in power when gas prices go up as being their fault, but when gas prices go down will equally loudly discount the opposition had anything to do with it. Remember this on *every issue*. Be not afraid to push falsehood.

It is not truth and justice your voters seek.

It is assurance that they are not to blame for anything & deserve better.

<u>Voters who actually seek truth and justice for all are not your voters and never will be.</u>

Ignore them, their needs, their voices, their concerns.

Weaponize ignorance.

Chapter 8

SIXTEEN AMERICAN ILLUSIONS

Do not attempt to educate those living under illusions. Use those illusions.

Throughout history, victors have pretended to worship local gods, hate local enemies, praise their people, and despise anyone different (whatever that may entail). Be flexible.

In your city, state, or region, find the local illusions clung to by the *most passionate voters*. Passion is what counts here. Irrespective of how wild or without any proof, if the crowd before you are passionate about an illusion, that is the illusion you should embrace.

ILLUSION	What Idiots Believe	How To Use It
Spygate	The Russian-collusion Narrative within our government, intelligence agencies, and many outside of our government all colluded to take down our elected President.	Use this as a "proof" of just how real Deep State is.
Mainstream News Media	They spin, manipulate, and out and out lie, owned by Deep State, operating with the CIA, and have propagated hoaxes and lies since their inception.	Claim they are dying a slow death and being replaced by your own "legitimate journalists and reporters" who cover "the real news."

Climate Change Hoax	To get us to pay more for "green" products and punish corporations whose leaders fight the 'Deep State.'	Quote contrary fringe articles and unsupported academic studies as though they were true.
Vaccine Industry	Those overseeing the vaccine industry weaponized it. From the false swine flu epidemic to the measles scare to change legislation, HPV causing deaths, thousands of reports of them causing autism & death.	Quote contrary fringe articles and unsupported academic studies as though they were true.

Health Industry	Falsified info creates fear to monopolize the industry, keep you sick, and line their pockets while holistic doctors are mysteriously dying. Big pharma equals big bucks.	Quote contrary fringe articles and unsupported academic studies as though they were true.
Child Protective Services & Foster Care	Those at the top have created these structures for kidnapping and trafficking children.	Quote contrary fringe articles and unsupported academic studies as though they were true.

Education System	It has been designed to indoctrinate children with disinformation, teaching them about fabricated historical events and pumping them full of false secular narratives, like evolution.	Support religious superstition over science. Recommend changes that put your local supporters in control of schools instead of trained professionals. Keep the cattle ignorant.
Taxes	Taxes are used to fund NGOs, foreign enemies, and a myriad of other things that never truly see the light of day because the money is pocketed.	Find unpopular programs (even those which use very little of the budget) and blame them for federal deficits.

Conspiracy Theory	The term was coined by the CIA to call out people who were honing in on exposing true conspiracies. They and the FBI have secret agendas against (white) Americans.	Support popular current conspiracies (Russia helps the Clintons, Sandy Hook never happened, Pelosi attack hoax). Evidence is not required as they already believe or want to.
Big Government	Wire fraud to money laundering, altering legislation, pay-to-play schemes, and child pornography, and dictating what you must allow to be injected into your children.	Accuse your opponents. Again, evidence is not required. Just claim that you have it or will soon release it.

Entertainment Industry	Hollywood's been tied to the CIA for decades, Disney's had its dark connections and pedophilia issues, and the Music Industry is filled with those propped up to brainwash the masses and push the agendas of those in power.	Use this to spread distrust in those who have the public eye, to discredit them. They have the money and position to be heard, so make everything they say a lie before they even say it.
Immigration	The democrat-Liberal goal is to continue so that America will be overrun with immigrants having babies, creating power over true whites and other Americans.	Touted the strategy of "Replacement Theory." So scary to the cattle that even the possibility of it being true is enough. "Gun control" means to disarm us.

The United Nations	One of the seediest organizations is the UN. They are behind the Replacement agenda and have been called out numerous times for rape, sexual misconduct, and pedophiles.	Use unrelated events like when Bill Clinton was made the UN special envoy to Haiti in 2010. Opponents cannot defend against or disprove a negative.

The Catholic Vatican	Supported by the Deep State, instead of supporting the victims and holding despicable priests accountable, the Pope said, "Accusers are friends or relatives of the Devil," shaming victims and saying, "he who loves the Church knows how to forgive."	American Christians already dislike, distrust, or outright hate Catholics, so use it.
Abortion and Planned Parenthood	Whites are at the lowest birth rate in 80 years. It is also about selling body parts, experimentation, big money, etc.	Accuse anyone spouting 'Pro Choice', like a Kamala Harris, as part of the cover-up.

Student Loan Forgiveness	A Democratic party staple, totaling $800 million under Biden in 2023, designed to secure young voters. It gives the illusion the Democratic party cares for people.	Point out students signed up for those loans & got a degree out of it. How about forgiving medical debt instead? It's less than $300 million and those people are just trying to survive? Fair is fair.

Chapter 9

POSTSCRIPT: TALKING POINTS

Who Are "They"?
· The Deep State, which stems from family bloodlines going back hundreds of years, has operated as a shadow government and has maintained power over everything in this report
· Factions within government departments
· Select groups within the CIA, FBI, and other 3-letter agencies
· Portions of Hollywood and the music industry
· Numerous philanthropists, billionaires, and operators of NGOs
· Many leaders and decision-makers in big universities
· Players in big pharma, the health industry, and scientists going along for the ride

- Representatives in political positions of power
- Many in law enforcement, military, the courts, all the way up to judges

What is it "They" Want?
- To perpetrate propaganda on the world to feed their agendas
- To control your mind, thoughts, desires, behavior, and beliefs
- To control your finances and your function in the world
- To strip you of your right to bear arms so they have greater control
- To reduce the population. "They," all say so themselves
- To one day replace you and your job with artificial intelligence (AI)
- To produce mass-scale hoaxes of great proportion to produce a stream of money to line all their pockets
- To own and control everything they can on God's green earth
- A new world order with a single global governance

THEY want it all. And, it is they, not we, who want you to be the sheep that serves them, keeps their businesses rolling, and be forced to give up a huge percentage of your taxes that flows through the government and into their hands. All the while, they - not we - keep you living paycheck to paycheck, so you don't have time to see the truth, nor the energy to dig for it. Be creative in fabricating these endeavors: your supporters will generate their own for you to embrace!

www.ingramcontent.com/pod-product-compliance
Lightning Source LLC
Chambersburg PA
CBHW031157020426
42333CB00013B/701